Life Force for Beginners

Experiments, Reflections, Contexts and Models

Contact: www.HarryEilenstein.de
Harry.Eilenstein@web.de
Harry Eilenstein at youtube

Production and publishing house: BoD – Books on Demand, Norderstedt

ISBN: 9783754304662

Table of Contents

1. Evidence of the Life Force

When speaking or writing about a thing, it is useful to first prove that this thing actually exists.

For the existence of the life force several methods come into question: telepathy, telekinesis, homeopathy, astral projection, acupuncture, acupressure, rang dröl, pranayama, consecrations, magic, astrology and some more.

Telepathy can be demonstrated quite easily: You put two dozen postcards each in an opaque envelope and seal it. Then four people (who do not know the postcards) put one of these envelopes between them, concentrate on it for three minutes and then write down their impressions.

From the perceptions that three or four of them had, they prepare a description of the picture, which they supplement with the perceptions that only two people had. The perceptions, which only one person had, are left out, because they may not have been telepathic perceptions, but an association or similar.

For the telekinesis there is an experiment, which one can see on the Internet, but which one should also carry out oneself, so that one sees that it really functions. In this experiment, which can be found on youtube under "Telekinesis Paper Wheel" or "PSI wheel", a paper wheel, which can turn almost frictionless on the tip of a pin, is turned by one's own imagination.

The effectiveness of homeopathy is not so easy to prove, because you need some own experience with it. In homeopathy globules are used, which are prepared in a special way: For example, for the sulfur globules, sulfur is mixed again and again with lactose until the sulfur in this mixture has been diluted so much that finally there is no sulfur left in the lactose. The globules then act like sulfur, but there is no more sulfur in them – the active ingredient is thus the life force of the sulfur that is still in the globules.

During an astral projection, one's consciousness and perceptive faculty are outside of one's physical body, which is usually explained by the fact that consciousness and perceptive faculty belong to the life force body, i.e. to the total life force that is in a human being. This life force body may temporarily leave the physical body.

In acupuncture, acupressure, rang dröl, pranayama and similar methods, there is only a small amount of physical energy acting. In the case of acupuncture, acupressure, rang dröl, pranayama and similar methods, there are only slight physical triggers for the achieved effect, so that one can also consider an effect in the area of the life force here.

During a _consecration_ an object changes its radiance and its effect. Since these effects are not physical but magical, and since nothing is physically changed in an object by a consecration, the effect must be in the realm of the life force. Two of the better known consecrations are the "charging" of a talisman and the consecration of the wafers and wine in the Christian Lord's Supper.

In general, almost all phenomena in _magic_ can be traced back to the life force or explained with it.

Since also _astrology_ describes non-physical connections, it's wuite probable, that it is also based on the life force.

If you know at least one of these phenomena yourself, it makes sense to read this book further – otherwise all further considerations would hang a little "in the air".

Through telepathy, telekinesis, homeopathy, astrology etc. it can be shown that there are non-physical connections. The life force is a possible explanation for this kind of connections.

2. A Model of Magic

What is the life force?

First of all, it is a model that has been used to try to explain a variety of phenomena.

A good model, which makes it possible to describe otherwise isolated phenomena with a simple basic assumption, is something quite practical – especially if one can draw conclusions from the model, which then prove useful in practice …

Finally, with every model it is important to keep in mind that it is a model, i.e. a description: One observes phenomena and looks for as comprehensive and simple a description as possible for all these phenomena – that is all the mind can do, and that is also exactly what a model is and can be.

But it is no small thing – if a good model can accurately predict what action will have what effect, it can be a great relief in daily life.

What do the experiments in the previous chapter suggest about the description of vital force?

In essence, it is first of all something that is directed by consciousness – more precisely, by concentration (will) and imagination (inner pictures).

This allows for a variety of applications:

- Life force can be sent – telepathy.

- It can be imprinted with information – telepathy.

- It can have a physical effect – telekinesis.

- The imprinting of the life force of an object can have a permanent effect – consecrations.

- The life force of a person is an image of the physical body – the life force body ("astral body").

- The life force body can leave the physical body, which in the end is nothing else than sending life force as in telepathy, only that here it is not a matter of sending mail, so to speak, but of traveling – an astral projection.

- The life force can be moved in the human body by acupuncture, acupressure, rang dröl, pranayama, etc., creating specific effects, which suggests that the life force in man is not a "homogeneous mist", but has an organized structure – the chakras and the Kundalini.

- Finally, astrology, which describes the relationship between the planetary position and events in the life of people, animals, plants, things, institutions, etc., indicates that all things contain life force, otherwise astrology (if based on life force) could not affect all things.

Since astrology also describes collective events such as revolutions and wars, the life force also seems to be organized collectively, i.e. to possess comprehensive structures that go beyond an individual being, since otherwise such collective effects would hardly be conceivable.

The life force seems to be something quite similar (or the same) as the collective subconsciousness.

The life force is thus a non-physical substance, which can be directed by humans and possibly also by the planets as well as possibly also by animals and plants.

It can transmit information as well as effects.

It can be sent (telepathy) as well as stored (consecrations).

The life force, at least of humans, but probably not only their life force, is structured and organized (chakras, kundalini) and can temporarily leave the physical body (astral projection), in which case the consciousness and the ability to perceive are bound to the life force body and not to the physical body.

Looking at these properties of the life force, one peculiarity of the name "life force" stands out: The life force is everywhere regarded like a "magic substance", but it is not called "life substance", but "life force". Obviously here is not distinguished clearly between "substance" and "effect of the substance".

Therefore, one could compare the life force with the energy quanta, which are both particles ("quanta") and forces ("waves") – which, of course, does not have to mean that the life force consists of energy quanta. It is worth noting, however, that the contradiction between the description and the designation of the life-force is reminiscent of the wave/particle duality in physics.

This reminds also of the fact, that every force constists of little particels, that move in space from one object to another – these particles are graviton, photon, gluon, W-boson, and Z-boson.

How does this striking contradiction between the description and the designation of the life force originate?

If one describes with the help of the life force e.g. the telepathy, life force is sent, so to speak; if one describes with the life force an astral projection or the effect of a chakra, one comes to the picture of a "second body" made of life force. Life force is therefore a substance.

However, if one describes with the help of the life force e.g. the telekinesis, one can understand this also as sending out of life force, but also as a "non-physical inter-action", thus as a force which goes out from the life force and moves a physical object. Thus, the life force has a physical effect, i.e., it emits a physical force.

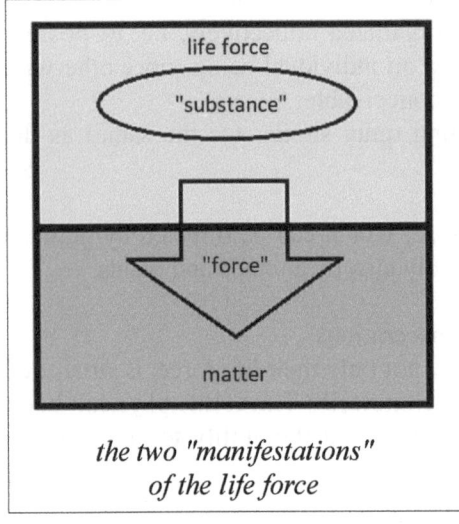

the two "manifestations"
of the life force

As long as one considers the life force in itself, it appears as a "magic substance" which is separated from the physical world. However, if one considers the effect of the life force in the physical world, it appears as a force which intervenes, so to speak, "from the outside" into the physical world.

Life force is thus statically regarded a substance, but dynamically regarded a force. Or differently formulated: As long as the life force remains on the "life force level", it appears as substance; however, if it takes up contact with the physical level, it appears as a force.

Interestingly, something quite similar is found with the wave/particle dualism in physics: A photon (i.e. a quantum of light) appears as a wave as long as it moves freely through space, is mirrored, changes its color or the like – you may say, as long as it "lives on" as light. But as soon as the photon hits an atom and is "swallowed" by it, i.e. increases the energy level of the atom, it behaves like a particle and gives this atom a kinetic impulse, i.e. a push.

Energy quanta behave like waves as long as they continue to exist as free energy quanta. However, as soon as they become a part of an atom, they have the properties of a particle.

In physics, the distinguishing criterion between the "wave character" and the "particle character" of an energy quantum is whether the energy quantum continues to exist – if so, it appears as a wave, if not, it appears as a particle. As long as an energy quantum continues to exist, it is free to oscillate and therefore appears as a wave; however, when the energy quantum dissolves into an atom or the like, all of its energy flows into the atom in question and therefore all of its energy appears as a particle (i.e., it gives the atom a "push").

The formulation of dualism is not identical in life force and in physics, but it is very similar. The dissolution of an energy quantum in a collision with an atom corresponds in the life force to the change from the "magic level" to the "physical level".

The "dualism of essence" in physics and magic		
	process	
	persistence	*dissolution / level change*
area *physics*	wave	particle
area *life force*	substance	force

It is noticeable that energy quanta, if they continue to exist, appear as energy – that life force, on the other hand, if it continues to exist, appears as substance. At first one could associate the wave, thus the "energy character" of the quantum rather with the force aspect than with the substance aspect of matter, but this equation is not as sure as it looks at first.

Since Einstein it is known that substance (mass) is a form of energy: $E=mc^2$. So it is fitting that the energy quanta in their appearance as wave, i.e. as energy correspond to the substance aspect of the life force.

In the same way, one could first associate the particle aspect of the energy quanta (substance, mass) with the substance aspect of the life force. But in this comparison there was a difference: If in physics an energy quantum appears as a particle, it has "died", it has collided against an atom and has become part of it, it has thus changed its form of existence, changed its sphere of life.

The same applies also to the life force: It appears as force only if it changes the level, thus from the "magic world" into the physical world.

Now, of course, in this consideration there is a snag: The wave/particle dualism of physics takes place completely in the physical world, while the substance/force dualism of the life force takes place in two worlds – i.e. in the physical world and in the "magic world".

The question arises whether the two forms of dualism can really be compared in the way suggested here. One can also argue that "particle", "wave" and "substance" are the same thing – just mass and energy respectively ($E=mc^2$). Force, on the other hand, is something quite different – you can turn mass into energy, but not into force.

If one starts from this view, one would rather compare the substance aspect of the life force with the particle character of an energy quantum and the force aspect of the life force with the effect of this energy quantum. Thus a photon, i.e. an energy quantum of the light, is on the one hand a particle, but on the other hand the photon also causes the electromagnetic force.

Is this comparison possibly more precise? At this stage of the investigation this cannot be said for sure – this occurs rather often in a research project …

9

So, first of all, one can only say that there is a dualism in physics as well as in life force, which has to do with the question whether the considered entity continues to exist in the process one is investigating or not.

Whether this result can contribute something for the understanding of the life force, is unclear with the state of the considerations in this chapter for the time being, but at least by these considerations a further characteristic of the life force, i.e. its substance/force duality, became clear – about what one (as a researcher) can be already be pleased.

Life force is most often seen as a milky-white fog that often has a slight blue touch.

One can ask oneself whether what one sees clairvoyantly is actually the life force itself or whether one does see that what contains the life force? Or does one see just contents of one's consciousness? Or is the milky-white fog of the life force simply a translation of an telepathic perception into an optical form?

With seeing there is the distinction between "light" and "seen object". In seeing, one generally perceives only light, but the form in which one perceives the light is always either a light source or an object that has reflected the light of this light source. By analyzing the rays of light that reach the eyes, the brain is able to deduce what objects are around oneself.

In this form, there is also the distinction between the "clairvoyant light" that one sees clairvoyantly and the object that one perceives through this "clairvoyant light".

So, on the one hand there is the ability of this clairvoyance and on the other hand there is what one perceives by this clairvoyance.

The generally usual assumption that what one clairvoyantly perceives consists of life force is therefore anything but certain.

One can only say that in clairvoyance ("life force seeing") one sees in a different way than with the physical eyes – possibly one only uses the life force to perceive things which themselves do not necessarily consist of life force. This "substance", of which the things one clairvoyantly perceives consist, could be either the physical things themselves or the life force of these things or just the consciousness of these physical things – this is still unknown for the time being.

Viewed in this way, the life force is no longer the "substance" of some kind of "parallel world", but merely a form of perception, or even more precisely, an aid to perception. The life force would then be an analogy to the light outside: a light within.

One could therefore suppose that life force is ultimately simply an "activity of consciousness" corresponding to seeing with the physical eyes.

Since the life force is also the means by which one can achieve telekinetic effects, this "activity of consciousness" corresponds not only to seeing with the physical eyes, but also to moving things with the physical hands.

There is one more property of the life force which could be considered in this context: Astral projections (sending out one's life-force body), telepathy and telekinesis show that the life-force is closely connected with consciousness – more closely than with the physical body, since the consciousness remains in the life-force body during an astral projection and not in the physical body.

Here another duality becomes visible: that of body and spirit, of matter and consciousness. One may at least have the justified initial suspicion that the life force is very closely connected with the consciousness. At least it looks like as if one could not understand the life force without a consideration of the matter/consciousness duality.

If one bases the consideration of the life force on the very simplest interpretation of this dualism, the life force would correspond to the consciousness. Telepathy would then be the sending out of a part of the "substance of consciousness" and telekinesis would then be the access of the consciousness to a substance outside of the own body, so to say an extension of consciousness, by which this substance outside of the own body can be temporarily directed in the same way as one's own body.

Whether this very simple model in this form is free of contradictions and therefore usable, will be shown in the further considerations.

The life force is a description model for non-physical connections.

The life force in this model is a non-physical substance or force, which can be directed by humans and possibly also by animals, plants and others. It can transmit information as well as effects. It can be sent (telepathy, telekinesis) as well as stored (consecrations).

The life force, at least in humans, is structured and organized (chakras, kundalini) and can temporarily leave the physical body (astral projection), in which case the consciousness and the ability to perceive is bound to the life force body and not to the physical body.

3. Life Force as a Description-Model of Magic

My "colleague" Frater U.D. once has summarized the different models of magic in a simple overview and distinguishes four different explanatory approaches:

- Magic is based on the life force, with whose help the magic effects are caused.

This model is well suited for the explanation of telepathy, Reiki, astral projection and the like.

- Magic is based on the help of ancestors, spirits, gods, etc., through which the magical effects are produced.

This model is well suited for explaining spiritism, family constellations, invocations, consecrations, miracles and the like.

- Magic is primarily a process in the psyche that produces the magical effects through an undefined process.

This model is well suited for the explanation of the depth psychology of C.G. Jung, the collectoive subconsciousness, sigil magic, "wishes to the universe" and the like.

- Magic is based on the exchange of information, with which the magical effects are also connected.

This model is well suited for the explanation of telepathy, Tarot readings, astrology and the like.

The first two models, i.e. the life force model and the spirits/gods model are the oldest and the most widespread. The other two models are from the last century.

However, these four models are ultimately not fundamentally separate, but four aspects of the same broader model based on an expanded description of the properties of the life force:

- If the life force 1. has a structure, 2. is connected with consciousness, and 3. can separate as a whole, e.g., from a human being (astral projection), then one should be able to assume that these structured, consciousness-filled and inde-pendent "life force organisms" correspond to the spirits and gods.

- The psychological model considers the contents of the psyche of man. However, since the psyche as the totality of the contents of a person's con-sciousness is largely identical with a person's life-force body (which contains

12

that person's consciousness), the psychological model is primarily a limitation on the consideration of the life-force contents and life-force structures of an individual person.

The collective subconsciousness of people would then be the total organization of the psyches of all people in a superordinate structure via telepathy.

- Since the life force can be imprinted with information (mostly images), the information model is primarily the consideration of the "postal shipping aspect" of the life force model. This model is, of course, inspired by PCs.

These four different magic models can thus be seen as different aspects of the life force model.

The pleasant thing about this in the context of this book is that these four models do not require any further assumptions of properties or the like of the life force and that the rather simple model sketched out in the previous chapter can be retained for the time being.

But astrology and the analogical order of things, so conspicuous in magic, cannot yet be explained with the help of these models.

Life force is a non-physical substance, which is closely connected with consciousness and therefore can also appear as astral bodies, spirits, gods and the like. It contains information and corresponds to the psyche.

---

4. Aura vision

In magic and among healers there is much talk about "life force" – how is it perceived at all? Or is it just an abstract concept?

There are people who can see the life force. This kind of perception is even described in a distinctly uniform way, regardless of the culture to which the person belongs: a milky white glow with a slight blue shimmer. Thus life force is sometimes called "white fog" or "smoke" or the like.

This phenomenon has led to the description of the life force body of the deceased as "bed sheet ghosts". This life-force body is most easily perceived around the head – which has given rise to the motif of the halo.

The animal deities like White Buffalo Woman, Great White Wolf, White Elephant and so on are called "white" because they consist of life force and appear therefore as figures made of luminous, dense, white fog.

Sometimes you can also see structures in the life force body – different color shimmers, color lines, rays, the chakras, the kundalini, etc. Apparently, structures within the life force body are also perceptible.

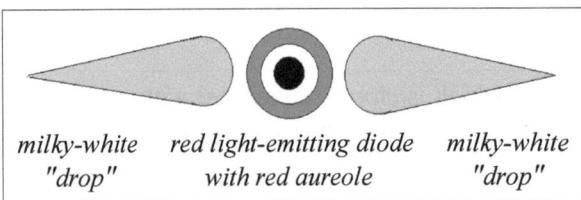

milky-white "drop"   *red light-emitting diode with red aureole*   *milky-white "drop"*

It seems that not only living beings have life force, but also some other things. Apparently the "aura seeing" is easiest with light emitting diodes – at least it is easiest for me there. Interestingly, a red light emitting diode also has a milky white aura (see my own perception in the sketch) – this color difference largely excludes an optical illusion. The reason for the drop shape of this aura is unknown to me – it is reminiscent of the two "jets", i.e. the two rays which in a galaxy project out into space from the center of the galaxy disk to two opposite sides (see photo on page 31).

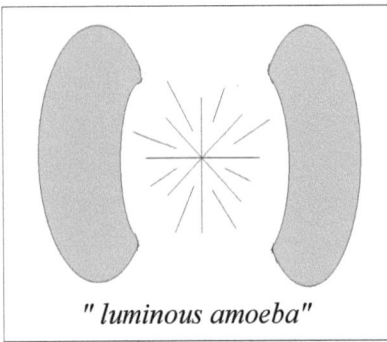

" luminous amoeba"

There seems to be also a vision from time to time, which consists of a kind of "luminous amoeba", which has the form of a bean and whose edge is frayed like felt. It also has this characteristic milky-white color with a slight blue tinge. Sometimes a second "bean" appears symmetrically to the first. Sometimes also a kind of "star" can be seen between them (see sketch).

However, these "luminous amoebae" are not

14

firmly bound to a place outside like the aura of the light-emitting diode, but seem to be coupled to one's own line of sight, which suggests an inner process – a perception of a part of one's own life-force body?

Seeing the life force is usually easiest at dusk, when the eyes can perceive little in the physical world.

Some people can feel the life force more easily than they can see it – usually as a kind of resistance that can be felt at a distance.

The perception of the life force as a vibration of mostly 6Hz also belongs to the tactile sensations.

Closely related to this is the perception of the life force as a difference in temperature, i.e. as a kind of "electric tingling heat".

One feels the "tingling heat" especially when one touches the aura, i.e. the edge of the life force body of another person. This is most easily felt when the other person is very active at the time, such as when dancing.

An extreme case of the perception of the life force as heat is the rising heat of the Kundalini.

The second form of perception (resistance at a distance) I experience especially during hikes in caves or in the forest at night, when one can see almost nothing.

Also still quite widespread is the "hearing" of the life force in "telepathic hearing", which can also be counted among the life force phenomena.

The sense of smell and the sense of taste appear only extremely rarely as a form of perception for the life force.

The visual perception of the life force seems to be the most widespread, while the tactile perception of the life force seems to be the type of perception that can be most safely awakened with some effort.

It makes sense to see which form of perception of the life force is the easiest for oneself – to make the learning of the perception of the life force as easy as possible.

With this observation something strange is noticeable: In the physical world pictures are perceived by seeing with the help of the eye, sounds are perceived by hearing with the help of the ear, objects are perceived by touching them through the skin, and so on. But this does not apply to the perception of the life force.

The life force is perceived by the consciousness as image, sound, touch etc., thus in the "language" of one of the physical senses. There is no independent perception of the life force, which would correspond to the seeing of the eye or the hearing of the ear. Obviously the perception of the life force must be "translated" into the language of one of the physical sense organs.

This leads to the suspicion that the perception of the life force takes place in a different way than the perception of the physical world. One has the impression that the various physical perceptions form a kind of "monitor" by means of which the life-force perceptions are mapped.

Instead, one could also say that the contents of the life-force perceptions are not built up from life-force, but from the smallest elements of the physical perceptions: from light, sound, touch, etc.

The human brain contains mainly optical information – therefore seeing life force as light ("clairvoyance") is the most widespread.

The sense of touch is very probably the oldest kind of perception – touching is the form of life force perception that apparently almost all people can learn. If you start a dream journey and you cannot see anything, it's almost always possible to touch the ground and feel if this is rock, sand, gras, wood and so on. From this touch-feeling you can then go on to the optical perception.

If one now sees this consideration in connection with the considerations in the two previous chapters, the impression arises that the contents of the life force or the perception of the life force would originate from the physical world, more exactly, from the elements of the perception of the physical world with the physical senses.

What do you actually perceive when you perceive life force? The contents of consciousness? Or a deeper layer of consciousness, in which, for example, there are no concrete images, but only light and color? Are these perceptions organized in some way?

A first clue is offered by a series of phenomena that can be experienced during meditation, dream journeys and similar "inner activities": There seem to be different forms of "inner seeing" – strictly speaking, there are five forms plus at least one more quite distinctive transitional form:

1. The outer world is seen by light coming from an external light source and reflected by objects.

2. In dreams and on dream journeys one usually sees shadowy images, which are partly "colored". The source of light is a diffuse, mildly bright "fog of light" that fills all places.

- As the meditation or dream journey deepens, individual symbols begin to become more colorful, glow slightly, and take on very sharp contours. In addition, images begin to flow constantly from one form to another.

3. At the next stage, one sees individual plain images of deep meaning, intensely glowing in color from within.

4. Next, one comes to a realm where one sees "contours in light," which are primal images like e.g. deities.

5. Finally, one can enter a realm consisting only of one glistening white light, that is everywhere and that ist the one, the all and the only.

These five ways of seeing plus the transition are also related to meditation systems and the like, such as the Kabbalistic Tree of Life, in which these five ways of seeing correspond to the five levels of Malkuth, Yesod, Tiphareth, Da'ath and Kether (together the "Middle Pillar").

At least, on the basis of this sequence one has the impression as if it could be true that the life force (or consciousness) is built up stepwise from an all-embracing One to the differentiated concrete – in the above-mentioned example thus from the "light in itself" to the perception of the pencil in one's own hand.

Life force does not have its own form of perception, but is perceived in the forms of the physical senses as image, sound, touch, heat, and so on.

Life force can also be perceived "object-free" as glistening white light – possibly corresponding to the inner "stillness" well known from meditation.

5. Traditional Concepts of the Life Force

If you look around in older cultures and in "nature-oriented cultures", you will find the concept of life force everywhere. The two best known names for the life force are probably the Indian "prana" and the ancient Egyptian "ankh".

Also, the concept of a life force body is found pretty much worldwide. Sometimes it is simply the "substance" of the soul, so to speak; sometimes there is a very differentiated system of various aspects of the non-material body.

Some of the differentiations are based on various symbols of the soul, as with the ancient Egyptians:

> - star ("Sa" body),
> - bird ("Ba"-body) and
> - life force ("Ka"-body).

Star, bird and life force are just three different pictures of the human soul – thus these three pictures don't describe three different aspects of the life force body (soul), but are just three different image-names of the soul.

In other systems, such as that of Theosophy and Anthroposophy, among others, the life-force body is differentiated on the basis of its capacities:

> - spirit (soul as that which has incarnated in man; consciousness),
> - astral body (feelings),
> - mental body (thinking), and
> - etheric body (life force).

So the these different non-material bodies are actually not different life force bodies, but merely distinctions of the abilities of the life force body.

So, for the time being, the life-force model still remains rather simple …

Widespread life force conceptions in almost all cultures are also the spirits of ancestors (ghosts), of animals (power animals), of plants ("elves") and of minerals (sometimes quite inaccurately called "dwarves") as well as the gods, although these are rarely expressly described as "life force beings".

Magic is also generally associated with the life force, which includes "magical healings."

Telepathy experiments with animals show (e.g. imagining a rabbit in front of a dog's snout) that animals also respond to telepathy and thus have a life force body. This is quite self-evident – for why and when should man have aquired a life force body?

The "talking with plants" and the "having a green thumb" show furthermore that also plants react to telepahty und thus have a life force body. In mythologies and religions these "conscious life force bodies" appear as "spirit beings": starting from the plant spirits over the power animals and the power animal mothers like the "white she-wolf" or the "white buffalo woman" up to the deities.

Even mountains sometimes have a "spirit" and a sea god is in a way also the "life force body of the sea".

The concept of life force is common throughout the world.
Life force is contained in everything and is often personified as a spirit or deity.
There are no traditional concepts of different types of life force, only of different manifestations of life force.

6. Traditional Properties of the Life Force

There are also properties of the life force that are often mentioned in mythologies.

The most important property of life force is undoubtedly vitality: A living being has life force – a dead being has no or hardly any life force. Therefore, a disease may also have been caused by a lack of life force.

The source of this life force in the oldest myths is usually considered to be the mother goddess. In the more recent myths, the sun god and later the king of the gods take her place, until finally the life force becomes an aspect of the One God, such as the Holy Spirit in the Christian Trinity.

The life force is often described as light or as fire, but this refers more to the perception of the life force than to the properties of the life force. However, with the help of the awakening of the Kundalini, i.e. the flow of the life force in one's own body, very real heat is also generated, with which, among others, the yogis in Tibet keep warm.

Another quality of the life force in the mythologies is "rightness". Strictly speaking, however, it is not a quality of the life force itself, but only a concept closely connected with it. This rightness is found, for example, as the sequence of the seasons, as the right sowing date, as the straightness of the axis of the potter's wheel, as the roundness of a wheel, as the being in tune of a harp, and so on. The source of this correctness is the security and the fullness with the mother goddess, from which then in the kingship the "good rule" of the sun god has become. Rightness is the "healthy state" and ideally also the "normal state" of the life force – which shows for example in the free, unhindered flow of the Kundalini.

But also every single human being has his rightness: the acting in harmony with one's own soul. This rightness is the central principle of order in the mythological-magical world pictures: the Ma'at of the Egyptians, the Me of the Sumerians, the Rita or Dharma of the Indians, the Tashi of the Tibetans, the Ho'zhong of the Navaho, and so on.

So the life force, when it flows in the right way, sustains life.

The life force sustains life, is closely related to "rightness" and is perceived primarily as light or heat.

---

7. The Deities of the Life Force

There is actually only one deity who primarily represents the life force: Shakti, the consort of Shiva. However, she is rather a secondary figure, i.e. a late personification of the life force of Shiva and not primarily a goddess in her own right, who brings the life force to the people or the like.

However, since the life force is closely connected with abundance as well as with nourishment, by which a part of the life force is taken inside the body and by which life is maintained, in the extended sense also the mother goddesses are life force goddesses – in particular those, which are represented with the nursing of an infant like e.g. Isis or Maria.

the sun-god, whose rays end in hands, that hold partly the Ankh (symbol of life)

If one extends the scope even further, one can also add the sun-gods, whose sun-beams are sometimes understood as the life force they send to the earth. The most known motive of this kind are probably the representations from the reign of Pharao Akhenaten, on which often the sun was represented, whose rays end in hands, which hand among other things the life hieroglyph "Ankh" to the Pharao.

One could also include the "cosmic Kundalini" among the life force deities, but since it is more a cosmological concept than a concrete deity, this would be rather far-fetched.

Partly there are also concepts of a life force level, which are quite old like e.g. the Yesod realm of the Kabbalah. However, these concepts have nowhere been worked out particularly clearly in the old mythologies.

What can be concluded from this conspicious lack of life-force deities?

Apparently, although the life force is a concept that has been around for a long time, it is not tied to any particular deity, but has formed a kind of background to mythology: Mythology describes processes in the realm of life force. However, the processes in the material world have not been so clearly separated from the processes in the inner, magical, mythological world.

The life force is in the myths, so to speak, as natural and omnipresent as the air.

The life force is a self-evident concept in the myths, but it is personified into a deity only in a few cases and then only late.

---

8. Chakras and Kundalini

The flow of the life force is a process that is often described. So it seems that this life force is not static, but dynamic. This means that the order associated with this life force is also not a simple, fixed distribution, but rather something like a certain oscillation pattern, probably variable within limits.

It would be interesting to know whether the life force moves in a certain way, that is, whether it has a certain dynamic. Unfortunately, not too much is known about this.

The flow of the life force in man has been researched most precisely so far. In man, the life force rises up inside the body, spreads out above the head, flows down again around the outside of the body, collects under the body, and then rises up again. This convection current ("circular current") is like a fountain: The water rises as a jet, forms a fountain at the top, falls back down as drops, and then collects again at the bottom of the jet to rise again.

The pump at the bottom of the jet of the fountain corresponds to the root chakra, where the kundalini can be awakened, which corresponds to the rising jet.

This life force ray passes through a total of seven chakras during its ascent in man, which can be understood as the organs of the life force body. The convection current of the life force including Kundalini would then be the blood circulation of the life force body.

The chakras, that is, these life force organs are polar and symmetrical around the heart chakra:

The Chakras			symmetry
Name	**Location**	**Location**	
crown chakra	parting	spiritual contact	
third eye	between the eyebrows	outer orientation	
throat chakra	middle of the neck	social self-expression	
heart chakra	chest center	identity	
solar plexus	just above the navel	physical self-expression	
hara	just below the navel	inner support	
root chakra	between genitals and anus	physical contact	

Between these main chakras are the minor chakras, which have the character of gateways between the seven main chakras. There transformations take place on the way from one main chakra to the other main chakra. In the following list the minor chakras are written in *italics*.

The chakras and the minor chakras		
Name	**Location**	**Property and function**
crown chakra	parting	spiritual contact
brow chakra	*hairline*	*orientation contact*
third eye	between the eyebrows	outer orientation
palatal chakra	*palate*	*authenticity becomes orientation*
throat chakra	middle of the neck	social self-expression
thymus chakra	*at the top of the sternum*	*identity becomes authenticity*
heart chakra	chest center	identity
wish tree	*at the bottom of the sternum*	*identity becomes wish*
solar plexus	just above the navel	physical self-expression
navel chakra	*navel*	*desire becomes attitude*
hara	just below the navel	inner support
pubic hair chakra	*upper pubic hair line*	*posture becomes encounter*
root chakra	between genitals and anus	physical contact

The minor chakras are also polar and symmetrical: The thymus chakra and the wish tree are located at the top and bottom of the sternum; the palate chakra is at the place where a person takes nourishment after birth, and the navel chakra is at the place where an unborn child takes nourishment; the forehead chakra is at the lower base line of the main hair, and the pubic hair chakra is at the upper base of the pubic hair.

There is another polar-symmetrical structure in the life force body: In addition to the vertical "main channel" of the life force in the center of the body, there are two other "channels" to the left and right of it in which the life force flows. The middle "channel" is called "sushumna" in yoga, the two outer ones "ida" and "pingala". The middle "channel" contains the image of the soul, the two outer channels contain the image of the whole inner man and the whole inner woman, respectively – so these two "outer channels" are polar-symmetrical not only in terms of their location, but also in terms of their quality, content, and function.

It seems as if polarity is an essential quality of the life force, because it appears in many places of this observation.

The system of chakras is even more complex, since there are also minor chakras in the arms and legs, among others, and since there is a subsidiary chakra ("gate") not only where the main "life force channel" (sushumna) goes from one chakra to the next, but also where the two subsidiary „life force channels" (ida and pingala) go from one chakra to the next. These many chakras and minor chakras make up most of the points on the body used in meditation, acupuncture, acupressure, Ayurveda, Rang Dröl, astrology (houses: body-zone analogies), etc.

If you look at all these body points from the different traditions together, you get a polar-symmetrical picture, which on the one hand is quite complex due to the large number of points, but on the other hand is again very simple due to the simplicity of the construction of this structure.

I have described this system in detail in my book "Das Chakrensystem mit den Nebenchakren".

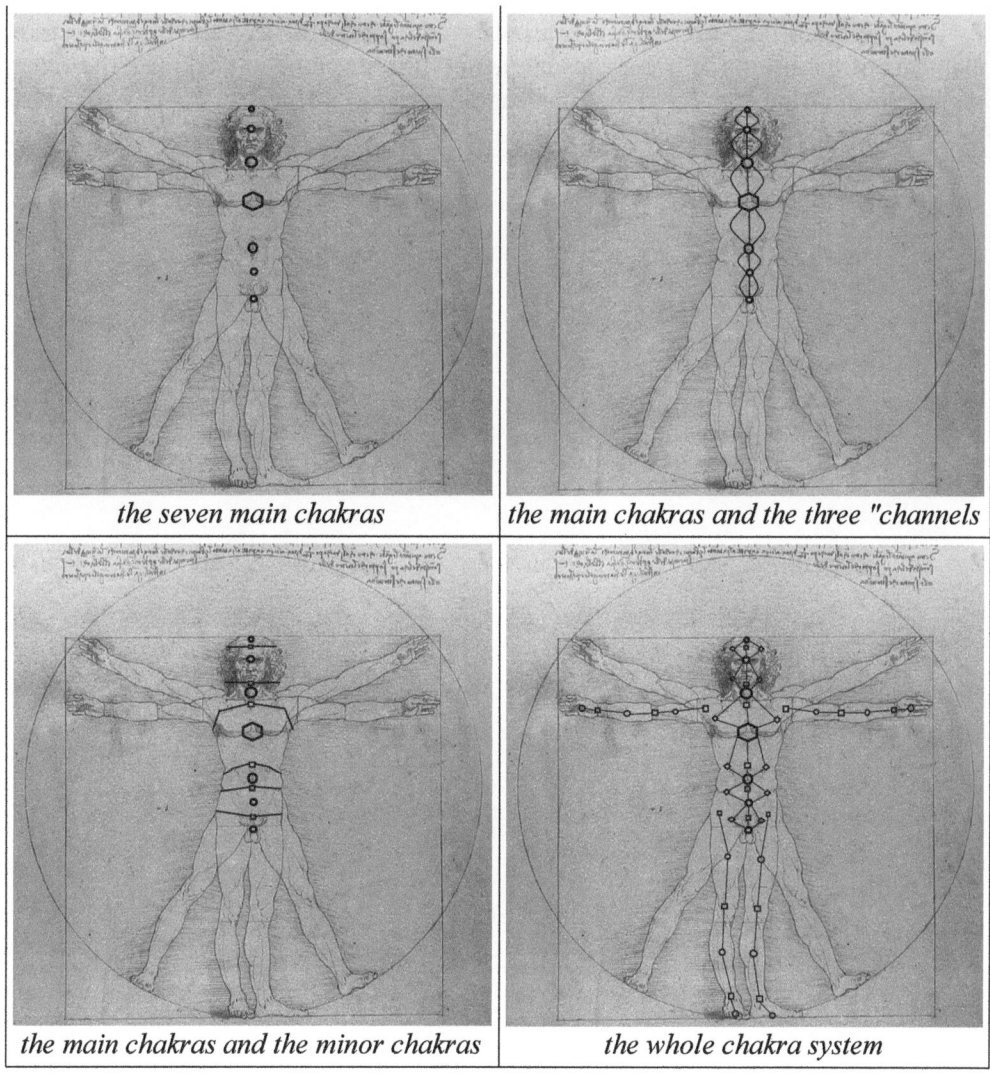

the seven main chakras	*the main chakras and the three "channels*
the main chakras and the minor chakras	*the whole chakra system*

The three peculiarities important for the study of the vital force, which have become clear in this consideration, are

    1. The tendency of the life force to form complex structures,
    2. the tendency of the life force to have a polar-symmetrical arrangement,
    3. the flowing in the form of a convection current.

The life force organizes itself in a polar-symmetrical structure. These structure elements of the life force in humans are mainly the seven main chakras ("life force organs"), which are connected by a convection current ("life force circuit"). A part of this circuit is the Kundalini.

9. Chakras, Stars and Vajra

The structure shown in the chakra system can be found in other places as well – it is most clearly visible in the structure of a sun, i.e. a star. As a symbol it is found as a Vajra in Indo-European religions.

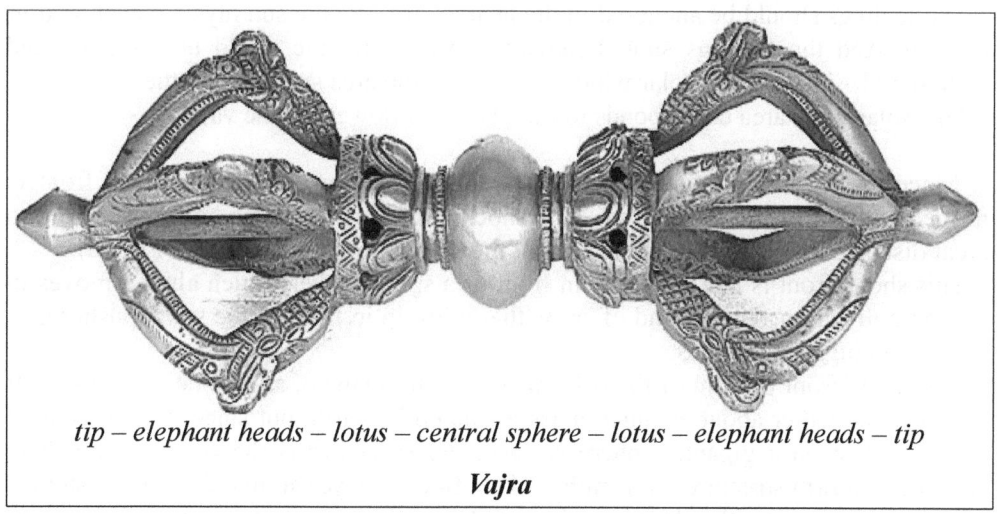

tip – elephant heads – lotus – central sphere – lotus – elephant heads – tip

Vajra

In the center of a solar system there is a star – in our solar system this star is called "Sun". The mass of this star is so big, that the pressure in the center caused by gravitation (contraction) is so high, that it "squeezes" the smaller atoms (hydrogen) together, thus forming bigger atoms (helium). Since in a helium atom more favorable energy conditions prevail than in a hydrogen atom, energy is released – the stars become "hot". The star then radiates this energy – the stars (and the sun as one of them) shine.

This star is the center of its system. It corresponds to the heart chakra as well as the sphere in the center of the vajra.

The sun emits not only light, i.e. photons, but also electrons and small atomic nuclei (of hydrogen and helium), i.e. ions. This radiation is called "solar wind".

Since this solar wind always has the same direction (away from the Sun), these photons, electrons and ions push away the fine stardust that is everywhere in a galaxy and thus also all around the stars (and the Sun).

A medium sized galaxy consists of about 100 billion stars (suns).

The solar wind leads to the fact that around the sun an area develops, in which the solar wind has pushed away the all the stardust, i.e. all foreign bodies (electrons, ions, fine rock dust) from the sun.

This area corresponds to the solar plexus and the throat chakra, whose activity is to implement the will of the soul in the heart chakra in the form of concrete desires, also removing all obstacles so that the desires become realizable.

The feelings of the solar plexus and the throat chakra are the emanations of the identity in the heart chakra – they are like the solar wind emitted by the sun.

The feelings should be anchored in the heart – just like the sun rays are anchored in the sun. And the feelings should radiate outward into the world unrestrained and unhindered – just like the solar wind radiates into the area surrounding the sun.

This solar wind area corresponds to the two lotus flowers of the vajra.

Since the solar wind pushes all the stardust away from the sun, a shock front is formed in front of the solar wind. This shock front forms a large hollow sphere at a great distance from the star (in the case of the sun, far outside the orbit of Pluto).

This shock front is like the snow in front of a snow pusher, which always moves in the same direction. The mound of snow that piles up in front of the snow pusher gets bigger and bigger as it goes.

The shock front in front of the solar wind has the shape of a huge hollow sphere. It contains altogether about as much mass as the entire earth, but since it is distributed as finest dust on a gigantic sphere surface, whose center is the sun, it is nowhere tangible as a firm structure – it is rather like a fine fog layer around the solar system.

Due to the constantly blowing solar wind, which presses against this shock front from the inside, this "nebulous spherical shell" expands more and more.

At the shock front the solar wind (the momentum of the star) meets the matter surrounding the star and forms a boundary region. This boundary region consists of the matter radiated by the star in the form of the solar wind, as well as the stardust encountered by the star as it passes through the galaxy to which it belongs.

In the same way, the impulses of the solar plexus and the throat chakra meet in their surrounding space, that is, in the hara and the third eye, the conditions in the world in which they want to realize the desires emanating from the heart chakra.

Where two different forces meet, a form always arises from the essence of these two forces. Thus, also from the impulses of the heart chakra of a person and from the momentum of the other people in his environment and the things in the world surrounding this person, the structures in the life of this person arise. This forming process can also be found inside the human being, when his genereal impulses (solar plexus and throat chakra) meet the world and let certain attitudes (hara) and ways of proceeding (third eye) arise on the basis of what they find there.

In the hara and the third eye the genereal impulses of the solar plexus and the throat chakra become specific impulses – e.g. the general wish of having sex becomes the wish of sex with a certain person.

This impact front corresponds to the elephant heads that emerge from the two lotus flowers.

When an object moves through another substance, a bow wave is created in front of that object in the direction of its movement – like the bow wave in front of a ship.

This bow wave is created by the ship bumping against the water molecules and these water molecules being pushed forward by the ship – just like a ball is pushed away when you kick it. If one would go along a way on which many balls would lie and one would kick against each ball, these balls would constantly fly away in front of one in the own movement direction and form a bow wave of balls.

Also the shock front in front of the solar wind causes a bow wave in the stardust by its constant, all-sided expansion.

This shock front corresponds to the establishment of contact, the first encounter with the outside realm – for which the root chakra and the crown chakra are responsible in the life force body of a human being. These two chakras are also the concrete contact with one's environment.

This area corresponds to the two tips of the vajra.

These analogies between the chakra system, the solar system and the vajra can also be represented graphically:

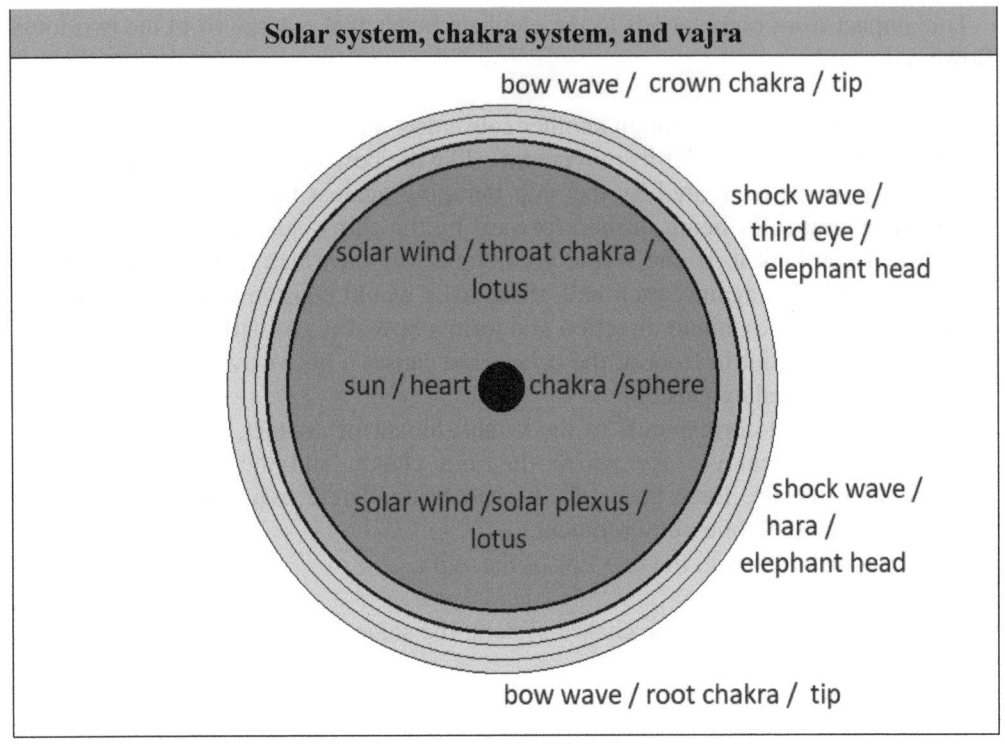

Solar system, chakra system, and vajra

bow wave / crown chakra / tip

shock wave / third eye / elephant head

solar wind / throat chakra / lotus

sun / heart chakra / sphere

solar wind /solar plexus / lotus

shock wave / hara / elephant head

bow wave / root chakra / tip

The sun contains many ions, electrically charged particles. As the sun rotates, these ions move. Moving electric charges generate a magnetic field, which is bundled at the poles of the rotating body and emerges there as a magnetic beam (magnetic north pole and magnetic south pole). This magnetic beam in turn captures ions and accelerates them so that they radiate out into space. These two beams at the two poles of a planet, a sun or a galaxy are called "jets".

When passing through the three areas (solar wind, shock front, bow wave), the two jets "above" and "below" the sun cause three vortices each, which correspond to the three chakras and, in the case of the vajra, to the lotus, the elephant and the tip. These two jets correspond to the sushumna in yoga, where the chakras are located, and to the two central rays of the vajra.

Since the positively charged ions and the negatively charged ions are accelerated in opposite ways, two spirals of particles are created around both magnetic jets, spinning in opposite directions. In yoga, they correspond to Ida and Pingala, which run next to the Sushumna (the central "channel" in which Kundalini flows).

The two magnetic rays of a galaxy ("jets")

Jets of a galaxy

Galaxy (the bright spot in the center) with two jets forming two very large red luminous clouds in the stardust surrounding the galaxy

The way in which a galaxy and a chakra system form correspond to each other in a very detailed way. The same forces seem to be at work in both, leading to the unfolding of these coinciding structures.

The resulting structure also corresponds to the structure of a vajra:

Sun, Chakras and Vajra		
Sun	Chakras	*Vajra*
Sun	Heart Chakra	Sphere
Solar wind space	solar plexus + throat chakra	two lotus flowers
shock front	hara + third eye	heads of elephants
bow wave	root chakra + crown chakra	tips of the vajra
magnetic jet	sushumna	two rays
two ion spirals	Ida + Pingala	pair of elephants

One may assume at least that the life force assumes this structure still at still more places. Probably this structure could be found also in the field of nuclear physics.

The exact agreement of the structure of the chakra system and a solar system lets assume that with both the same forces are at work.

31

Basically this structure results in relation to the solar system and therefore probably also in relation to the chakra system from the working of the three basic forces, thus

1. from the strong interaction ("color force") in the atomic nuclei, which causes e.g. the shining of the stars by the nuclear fusion;
2. from the electromagnetic force ("light"), which causes, among other things, the rays (jets; sushumna, ida and pingala); and
3. from the gravitation, which leads to the fact that the particles and the energy in the universe is not completely homogeneously distributed, but forms stars.

The three basic forces differ among other things by their polarity:

1. The gravity is unipolar, i.e. there is only one orientation of this force: gravity pulls all things together.
2. The electromagnetic force is bipolar, i.e. there is a "+" and a "–", which together result in the neutral state ("0"). Here, like repels like, while unlike attracts each other.
3. The color force is three-polar, i.e. there is a "red", a "blue" and a "yellow", which together give the neutral state ("white"). Three particles with these three colors form an indissoluble unit.

Of these three forces, so far in this book mainly the polarity, i.e. the correspondence to the electromagnetic force has been considered in the area of the life force: Yin and Yang, male and female, the two rays of the heart chakra (that form the sushumna), and the like.

The gravitation finds its correspondence in the fact that there are objects at all, since the gravitation leads to the fact that atoms are clustered together to stars. Accordingly, also the clairvoyantly perceived objects should have originated by a force corresponding to the gravitation. Maybe the tendency of inner images to form complex symbols could be seen as a correspondence.

With the color force it is more difficult to find it in the area of the life force. Most likely it should be assumed in the heart chakra, because this chakra is the center of the chakra system and corresponds to the sun.

The bipolarity of the life force is by far the most obvious and the most sure polarity of the life force. Whether there is also a one-polarity or a three-polarity in the life force is quite uncertain.

One can interpret the considerations of the complex structure, which is found in the life force body (chakras) and also in a solar system, in two ways:

> On the one hand, as two parallel worlds coupled to each other and formed by the same forces – a physical world and a life force world;
> and on the other hand as two different perceptions of the same world – once from the outside with the physical eyes and once from the inside with the consciousness.

According to the previous considerations, the second model, i.e. "two kinds of perception" would be the more probable and also the simpler one.

Ultimately, this would mean that one has two possibilities of perception and action:

> 1. the perception from the outside with the sense organs and the acting from the outside by the hands;
> 2. the perception from the inside with the consciousness ("telepathy") and the acting from the inside with the consciousness ("telekinesis").

This second form of perception and acting is what is commonly called "magic".

In normal perception and action, consciousness uses only one's own body and its possibilities; in magical perception and action, however, consciousness expands to what one wants to perceive or influence. In magic, the consciousness expands, it occupies the surrounding space, it expands to what it wants to perceive and direct.

This process can be easily experienced – it is virtually the central element in magic: in telepathy, one expands one's own consciousness to what one wants to perceive; in telekinesis, the thing, that one moves by telekinesis becomes a part of one's own body, so to speak, by expanding one's consciousness to this object, whereby one can then move this object like one's own hand; in hypnosis, one displaces the waking consciousness of the other person from his body, whereby one can then direct the actions of the other person oneself; etc.

What is the life force in such a model? Actually only an auxiliary function, a helpful image, with which one describes the contents of one's own consciousness, which appear when one goes with the consciousness beyond one's own body and then perceives, touches and directs other people, animals and things "from within".

Thus, the difference between normal seeing and clairvoyance is that in normal seeing the consciousness uses the physical eyes and in clairvoyance it extends one's consciousness to what one wants to perceive.

Life force is thus neither a substance nor a force, but the direct perception of another being or object "from within," that is, "from consciousness to consciousness." That which appears in clairvoyance as the substance aspect of the life-force is the direct perception "per consciousness" of another being or object (telepathy); and that which is perceived in clairvoyance as the force aspect of the life-force is the direct directing "per consciousness" of something which does not belong to one's own body (telekinesis).

> The life force forms a complex, polar-symmetrical structure that appears in humans as the chakra system. The same structure is found in the structure of the surroundings space of a star. As a symbol, this structure appears as a vajra.
>
> This structure is probably based on the three basic physical forces, which seem to exist in analogous form in the realm of the life force.
>
> This very detailed correspondence of the structures in the realm of the life force and in the realm of matter suggests that the life force is an "inner perception of the world":
>
>> The life force is the description of the world as it looks ehen seen directly from the consciousness – when one inwardly extends one's own conscious-ness to another being or thing and then perceives it (telepathy) and, if necessary, can move this thing like one's own arm (telekinesis).

10. Perception and Directing of the Life Force

One can take a closer look at how one can perceive the life force and how one can direct it. It would probably be more accurate to say instead "how to perceive and direct things in the realm of the life force."

The two terms that one finds in this context in pretty much all of the magical literature are "will" and "imagination."

Imagination

Imagination is the mostly pictorial vision, that is, the ability to inwardly picture an image, build a geometric structure, or hear a word, smell a fragrance, feel an object, sense heat, and so on. Imagination is therefore the counterpart of perception.

In perception, one sees an object with the help of the physical eyes and light, which then appears in the consciousness as perception. In telepathy, one sees an object directly by one's own consciousness.

In imagination, one creates the image of an object in one's consciousness with the help of the life force, which then produces a magical effect in the physical world.

The two processes are an exact mirror image of each other:

    1. perception: object => light => eye => image in consciousness.

    2. imagination: consciousness => image => life force => material effect

If one turns the terms in the second line, this analogy becomes even clearer:

    1. perception: object => light => eye => image in consciousness.

    2. imagination: material effect <= life force <= image <= consciousness

The external object corresponds to the material effect,
the light in the outside corresponds to the life force (usually seen as milky-white luminescence) in the inside,
the eye in the outside corresponds to the image in the inside,
and the image in the consciousness corresponds to the imagining consciousness.

This gives the impression as if both processes would take place in the same framework, would go the same way, only that the starting point with both is at the opposite ends of this way.

The physical and magical perceptions and actions can be represented altogether in a quite simple way. All processes are seen from the point of view of "person A":

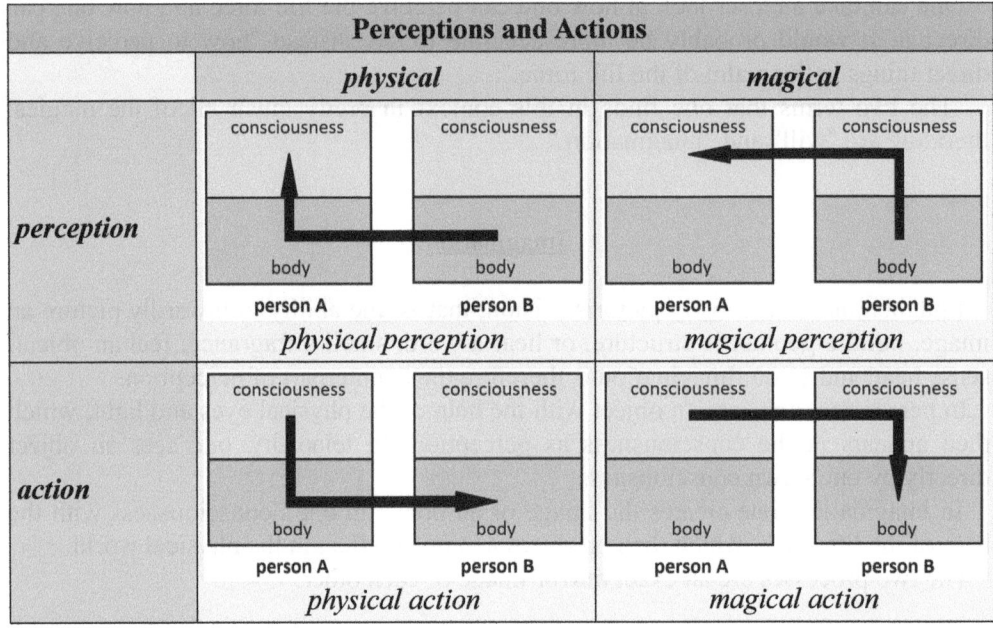

In these diagrams "person A" is the acting person and "person B" is the person who is seen or with whom something is done.

  - In physical perception, the contact takes place on the physical plane and then person A becomes aware of person B.

  - In physical action, the contact also takes place on physical level – the action is decided in the consciousness of person A and is then directed physically towards person B.

  - With the magic perception the contact takes place on the consciousness level. In the extension of the consciousness of person A to person B, the perceptions of the body of person B by person A appear to person A as life force.

  - In the magical action, the contact also takes place on the level of consciousness. In the extension of the consciousness of person A to person B, the imaginations of person A appear to person A as life force, which subsequently exerts an effect on person B's body.

Thus, the life force appears at the direct transition from consciousness to consciousness – "life force" is a term for the direct perception in the realm of consciousness as well as for the deeds in the realm of consciousness.

The life force is not a "parallel world" to the physical world, but is the structures and dynamics within the consciousness. With the help of these structures and their perception, creation and guidance, magic is practiced.

The life force can be recognized with the help of a diagram quite simply as the "form of the perception and the acts of the consciousness":

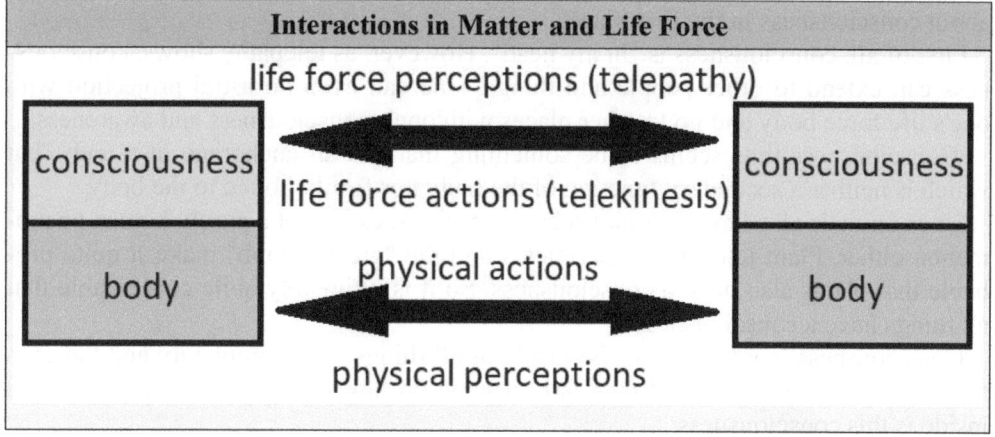

Will

The second important concept in magic is the will. While it is intuitively clear what "will" is, what is will exactly?

First of all, "will" is clearly more active compared to "perception". It is connected with the core of one's personality. It is the starting point of actions. It is what gives rise to independence. It is the source of a person's radiance. It is the starting point of a person's power and effect.

The "will" has a strange characteristic: every time you want to define it, you have to go back to its effects in order to call it the origin of these effects. But what is it itself?

One could also paraphrase the will as the effect of one's own soul in one's own psyche and in one's own body, but by doing so one has only shifted the point from which the effects of the will emanate one layer further back or inward again.

The will does not seem to be able to be defined causally, that is, not as something that has a certain property and therefore a certain effect. The will is always that from which an effect proceeds.

If you take a closer look at this last sentence, it is actually quite interesting, because doesn't it mean that the will is free?

If this conclusion should be correct, the question arises, where actually the origin of this freedom lies, if in the physical world nevertheless all things are causally defined – actually there should be then nothing in the physical world, which is free.

The will is at least in the subjective perception closely connected with consciousness. Possibly, therefore, more can be found out about the will, if one looks at the consciousness more exactly. Consciousness is also difficult to define, although everybody knows that it is there – without consciousness one could not ask the question about consciousness in the first place.

First of all, consciousness is "in my head". However, as telepathy shows, consciousness can extend to other people and things. One can even do astral projection with one's life force body and go to other places with one's consciousness and awareness.

Consciousness thus seems to be something that has an anchorage in a body, but which is neither a secondary function of the body nor firmly bound to the body.

Since animals also have consciousness, consciousness is not a purely human phenomenon either. Plant telepathy experiments and the "green thumb" make it quite probable that plants also have a consciousness. So it is ultimately quite conceivable that all things have a consciousness.

Consciousness would then be the inside of all things. The complexity and the contents of consciousness would then only depend on how complex the thing is whose inside is this consciousness.

If one thinks this finding further, it is well conceivable that the consciousness of all people is based on a total consciousness: the collective subconsciousness. If also every animal and plant species should have such a collective subconsciousness, it becomes ultimately conceivable that there is also a consciousness encompassing all beings and things, which one could most likely call "God".

This results in a kind of "family tree of consciousness":

- God: the all encompassing consciousness
- Deity: the consciousness of a certain principle
- Soul: the consciousness of an incarnation sequence
- Psyche: the subconsciousness of a human being
- Body: the normal waking consciousness

First of all, this family tree is quite abstract and may seem a bit arbitrary. However, it describes many experiences one can have while meditating and on dream journeys as well as in magic:

- The "consciousness in the body" is the normal here and now.

- The psyche is above all the subconsciousness of a human being. There, among other things, the imagination takes place.

- The soul is what has incarnated in a human being and what has created the psyche. It can also be understood as the source of the will, which shows itself in the psyche as impulses for action.

- Every soul has a protective deity: a deity that is, so to speak, a sea of which the soul is a drop. Therefore, one can assume that the will of the soul comes from the deity by which it was created.

- The same is true for the deities, which are aspects of the One God: The will of the deities comes from God's will.

But why should God have a will? If God is the One-All-Only, that is, the all-encompassing Consciousness whose body is the material world, then there is nothing besides God that could limit Him in any way – therefore God is free. This freedom would then ultimately be the origin of the will in man.

This freedom could then also be the origin of magic, because this freedom would mean that one can also shape the world freely – to the extent that one can clearly direct one's own will towards a goal.

At the root of the matter the causality, thus determination of all things is found – at the root of the consciousness, however, freedom is found. This fundamental difference presumably lies in the fact that matter is a great multiplicity in which so to speak "rules of development" have formed, while consciousness, if it should ultimately be the unity of God's consciousness, is just a unity and not a multiplicity.

Now this is of course everything else than a conclusive proof, but nevertheless a model, in which both the causality and the freedom have a place. The radiation of this freedom into the material world is the individual will. The consequent utilization of the possibilities of this will is magic – it can lead from simple telepathy over telekinesis to materializations.

In the end, nothing is impossible – or, as Christ said: "faith can move mountains" – whereby in this context "faith" is nothing else than the combination of will and imagination.

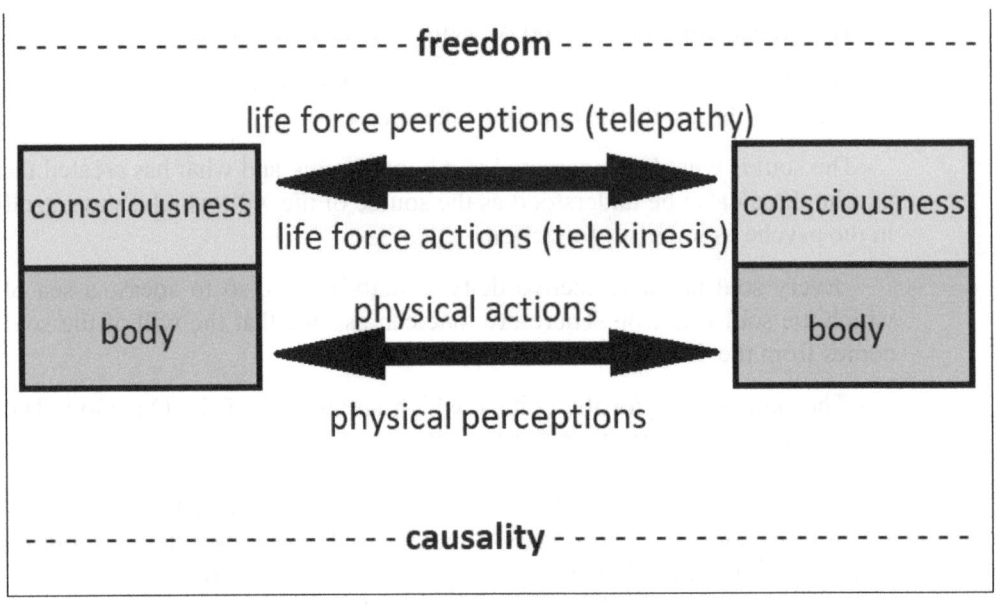

As already said, this model does not prove anything, but it describes in a very simple way the phenomenon of the life force as well as the possibilities of magic. Magic is nothing else than the free creation of one's own life circumstances – for which, however, the ability to will something and to be able to imagine it sufficiently clearly is necessary.

However, there is a "shortcut" in magic: If you are completely convinced that something is "right" and that you want it to happen, then it will happen. The life force, i.e. one's own consciousness then moves unhindered exactly in such a way that what one feels to be right also happens.

The explanation, which arises from this model for the fact that there is both freedom and causality, is quite simple:

> If there is only one Something, that Something can only be free, since there is nothing to constrain it – that is God as the all-encompassing Consciousness and as the root of freedom. "God" is conceived here as the One-All-Only, precisely as the foundation of the consciousness side of the world, the comprehensive inside of everything that exists, so to speak. A rather neutral-technical term for this One-All-Only, which comes from the Kabbalistic Tree of Life, is "Kether" ("Crown"). The definition of this One-All-Only, which belongs to this more technical term, is the God name "Eheieh" from the Old Testament – it means "I am I".

The material world is causally ordered for a very simple reason: It consists of such a large number of particles (from quarks to protons and atoms to dust grains, cells, people, and stars) that, because of their properties, they collectively form a "common flow," so to speak, out of habit and inertia. The inside (consciousness) of all these many units has thereby hardly a creative and therefore free influence. These units all constantly bump into each other, so to speak, which results in a very simple "dance" – just the causality.

On the basis of this consideration, the graphic shown on the previous page can be supplemented once again:

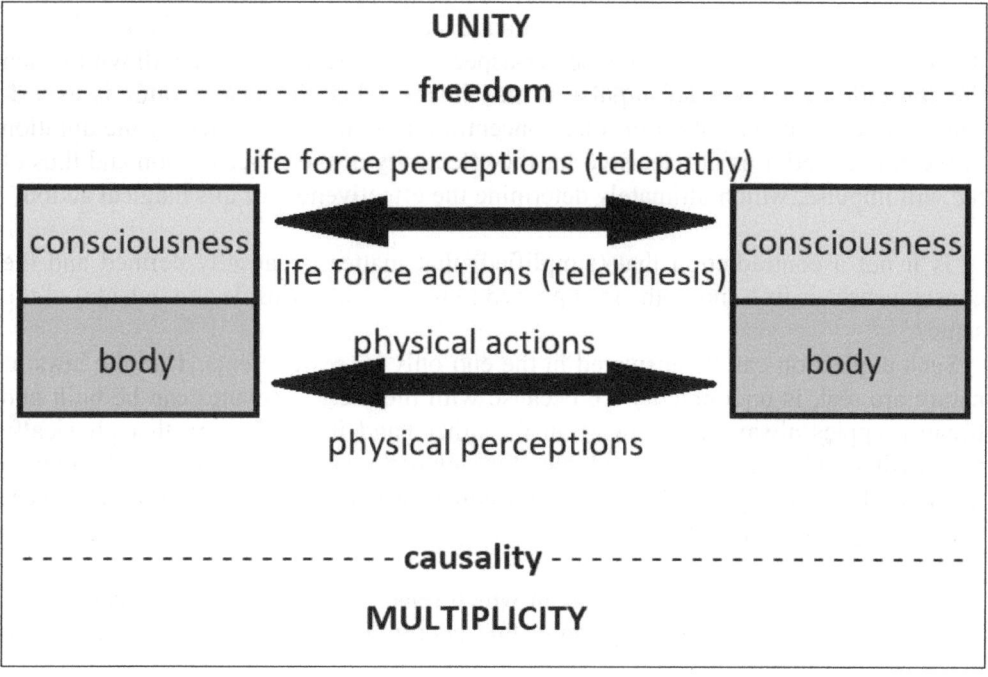

The above mentioned five-part "family tree of consciousness" also corresponds to the five-part sequence of the different kinds of perception of light, which has already been presented in an earlier chapter:

- God   = white glistening light
- Deities   = contours in the light
- Soul   = image shining from within
- Psyche   = images in a mist of light
- Body   = things illuminated from outside

41

Now what is the exact relationship between the will and the imagination?

The will is the impulse of action or creation, which comes out of one's own freedom.

Imagination is the (magical) creation of the desired state on the outside in the form of an image on the inside.

The imagination is the image of the goal – the will is the force that creates this desired goal in the outside.

The life force occurs in this context in imagination: One creates an inner image "out of life force," which in turn "directs life force," whereby it creates the desired goal in the outside.

The life force is to be seen here as "substance" and as "power": The substance aspect of the life force is the imagined image and the force aspect of the life force is the realization of this image. This power-aspect of the life-force is the will with which the consciousness gives an impulse to this image. This "impulse-giving" is experienced subjectively as a short or long concentration on the goal, whereby the duration of the concentration is not decisive for the effectivity of the concentration and thus of the will impulse, which ultimately determine the effectiveness of this magical action.

Is it not a contradiction that (simplified) that matter is causally defined and the consciousness is free and both are supposed to be two sides (inside and outside) of the same?

Such a question can be answered in the end only by experiments. That the laws of nature are real, is undoubtedly so, because with them e.g. airplanes can be built and because apples always fall down. On the other hand it is also sure that physically inaccessible information can be obtained by telepathy and that objects can be moved in a non-physical way by telekinesis. Consequently, one can state first of all that there is obviously a duality of perfect determination of matter and of freedom of consciousness.

Thus the more precise question is, in which relation these two stand to each other. First of all one can say a little slangy that everything runs causally, as long as no magician interferes …

A little more stately formulated this determinacy/freedom duality means that everything runs causally as long as nobody makes use of the freedom inherent in himself and sends with the help of will (free creation impulse) and imagination (creation of a consciousness picture of the desired result) a creative impulse into the world which becomes the cause of a causal development in it.

It should be noted that this is not only a matter of obtaining information or moving a feather, but also materializations are possible and such miracles as raising the dead. Of course, these miracles are available to a person as a real possibility only if that person has already experienced them – until then, such forms of magic are only imaginative fiction for the time being.

These considerations also show why positive thinking is so important: If one thinks inwardly constantly out of fear of something what one wants to avoid, one imagines a picture of that what one does not want, and charges it by the high concentration of the fear, so that it becomes a creation impulse – and happens sooner or later.

- - -

The diagram used here also makes it possible to graphically represent the four magic models of life force, spirits (ghosts, deities), psyche and information mentioned in an earlier chapter:

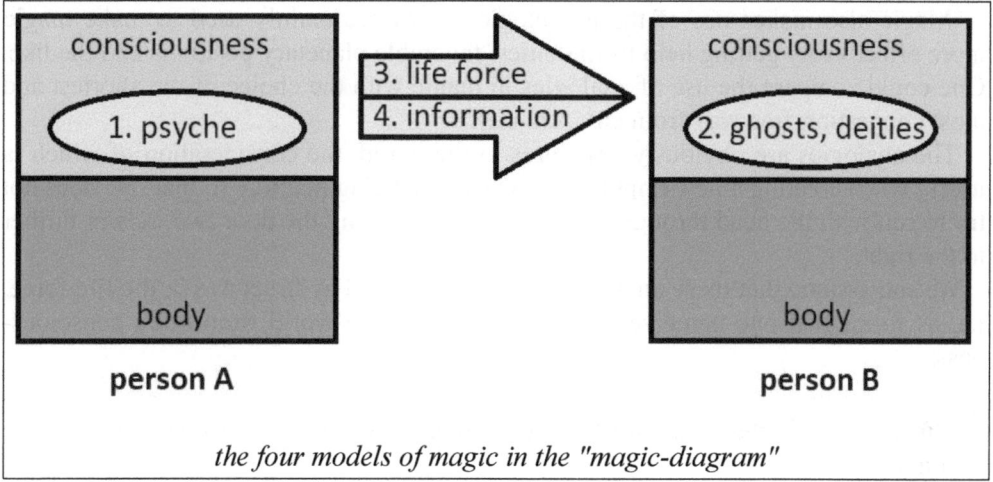

the four models of magic in the "magic-diagram"

- - -

As a conclusion of these considerations about "will and imagination" here follows an example of a magic action, in which will and imagination are clearly recognizable.

When I was a few years ago once with an acquaintance and helped her with the renovation, I needed a cordless screwdriver. She said that her boyfriend had left her one, but that it no longer worked. I tried it out and realized that it really didn't work anymore.

So I sat down, held the cordless screwdriver in front of me and "looked" into it, looking for a spot that felt funny. Finally, I found one that felt like a contact was broken at that point. Then I concentrated on that spot and imagined a ray of light ("life force") there, which reconnected the two sides of the broken contact. Since then this cordless screwdriver works again.

So life force and magic is not just a vague theory, but something distinctly suitable for everyday life.

Analogies

Then there is a third concept, which plays a big role in connection with magic and therefore could also be important for the understanding of the life force: the analogies.

It seems as if the world is structured not only causally, but also analogically. This is most obvious in astrology: a person's character and lifestyle is analogous to the position of the planets at the time of his birth, which is expressed through his horoscope. The same connection is also found in all oracles and omens.

Magic also makes use of these analogies. They are mainly used to make magic more effective by getting help from deities, favorable planetary positions and the like. One could compare the use of analogies in magic with the choice of the shortest and most congestion-free way from city A to city B.

The analogies are obviously structures in the world, the consideration of which is useful when creating a new impulse, i.e. when practicing magic – so that one does not try to run with the head through the wall instead of using the door two meters further to the right.

We can assume that these analogies can also be found as structures in the life force, i.e. as forms that one perceives when looking into the world from one's consciousness.

Imagination is the creation of an inner image, which then receives an impulse through the will.

Will is an inner freedom whose root is ultimately God's freedom – or, more abstractly, whose root is ultimately the unity of consciousness underlying all consciousness.

Imagination is the counterpart to perception: With perception, one sees something in one's consciousness that is already there outside – with imagination, one creates an image in one's consciousness that then becomes reality outside.

The analogies are a structure, which is found in the area of the consciousness and secondarily also in the physical world. These analogies should be taken into account in magic in order to take the easiest way to one's goal.

The life force appears at the border between the determinacy of the material world and the freedom of the consciousness. However, it is not an independent substance, but the direct perception of the consciousness and its contents.

---

11. Consciousness and Matter

In this book, on the basis of the consideration of the life force and the magical phenomena described by it, a model has been sketched in which the world has, so to speak, two sides, an inside and an outside, the outside being the material world completely determined by causality and the inside being the free world of consciousness.

The question now arises in what way this inner world and this outer world are related to each other.

First of all one can say that this is still quite unclear. But one can nevertheless make some considerations about it. One of them comes from the superstring theory of the physicists.

A superstring can be imagined as a vibrating string that forms a circle. For example, a proton (p^+) is such a vibrating circle.

The analogy to a superstring ist the zodiac: the simplest superstring and the zodiac are both like a vibrating string that has the form of a circle. This vibration has the form of a twelve-part "stationary wave".

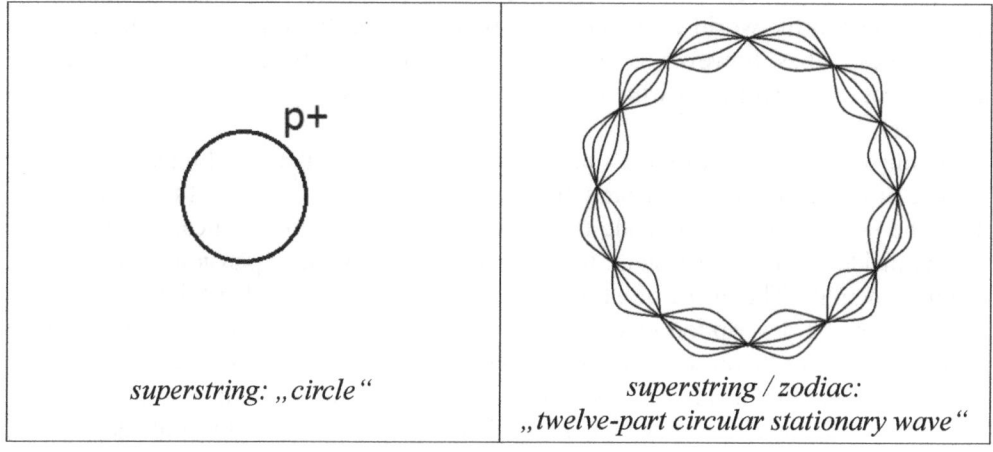

superstring: „circle"   *superstring / zodiac:*
„twelve-part circular stationary wave"

If one imagines now that such a superstring (here a p^+) moves, one receives the picture of a tube with the graphic representation of this temporal process. The time runs in the graphic from left to right.

If one has now two superstrings which attract each other, e.g. a proton (p^+) and an electron (e^-), then this can be represented as the exchange of a photon (energy quantum of the electro-magnetic force). A photon is also a superstring. The exchange of the photon (ph) appears graphically as another tube running from the proton to the electron.

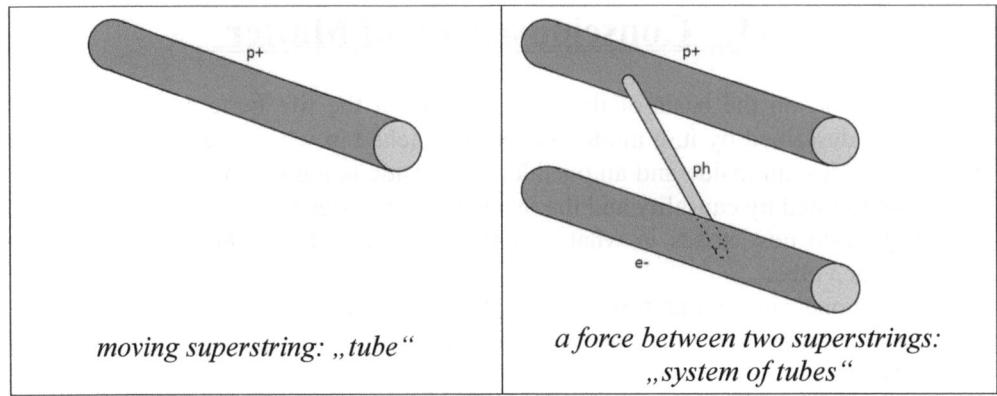

moving superstring: „tube"

a force between two superstrings: „system of tubes"

One can, so to speak, "walk" from the proton tube (p^+) through the photon tube (ph) to the electron tube (e^-).

In this way all material processes can be represented as a complex tube system.

In this tube system there is an "outside" and an "inside". The outside of the tubes can bump against each other and remain separated – this would correspond to the matter aspect of the world with its delimitation and determinacy (causality). The inner side of these tubes, however, is unlimited – they would correspond to the consciousness aspect of the world, in which one can move freely everywhere (from one tube to the other).

Of course, the outside of these tubes is also unlimited – there is ultimately only one surface of this endless, widely branched tube system – but in contrast to the inside of this tube system, on their outside there are collisions as "communication principle". On the inside of this tube system, however, there is only the expansion as "communication principle". The inside of a tube expands to the inside of other tubes.

This is only a description model, which is based on the today usual representation of the superstring theory (a so-called "Feynman diagram"), but it describes even the experiences on the inside and outside of the world quite well: a multiplicity of impacts on the outside, by which altogether a "steering from the outside" results (causality of the matter) and an expansion from the inside, by which a "steering from the inside" results (freedom of the consciousness).

Since the inside of a tube is connected with its outside, an inner movement (consciousness) is also an outer movement (matter) – in this way one moves e.g. one's own hand.

But if it is possible to extend one's own consciousness beyond one's own body, then one can also move other things and beings from one's own consciousness like one's own hand.

Why then is there a limit to the outside – also for the normal consciousness? It is obvious that, on the one hand, one's own body is also materially a self-organizing organic entity, and that, on the other hand, there are many more "connecting tubes" within the body than from the body to the outside. These "external connecting tubes" consist almost only of gravitons (gravity) and of some photons (electromagnetic force). Inside the body there are a lot of "photon-tubes, because the molecules and thus the cells are hold together by the electromagnetic force. Therefore it is quite plausible that one must take a certain effort to be able to move also something which is outside of one's own body like one's own hand.

Maybe it is no pure coincidence, that it is the electromagnetic force that holds the atoms in the molecules, the molecules in the cells, the cells in the organs and the organs in the body together – the electromagnetic force consists of photons and photons are light … and the clairvoyant perception of the life force ist a milky-white light …

The life force in this model is what the consciousness perceives when it moves outward beyond its own body to other things and beings in its surrounding space. These perceptions are all on the inside of the tubes, that is, in the realm of consciousness.

The physical eyes however lie on the outside of these tubes, they perceive the photons which hit the eyes from the outside.

The model represented here describes magic and physical phenomena quite well, but whether it is also really already correct in such a way as it was represented here, must still turn out. At least from this model first of all no contradictions arise to the observations – what is already very pleasing.

Matter is the outside of the world – it is causally defined.
Consciousness is the inside of the world – it is free.
The life force is what one perceives when one extends one's own consciousness beyond one's own body and perceives other things and beings from the inside, that is, from consciousness.

12. The Overall Organization of the Life Force

The life force has the tendency to organize itself in complex structures – such as the chakra system.

The "tube model" presented in the previous chapter, which comes from superstring theory, suggests that all things are interconnected. This assumption is also confirmed by the following consideration from physics:

- All matter is made up of molecules.
- All molecules consist of atoms.
- All atoms consist of atomic nuclei and electrons.
- All atomic nuclei consist of protons and neutrons.
- All protons and neutrons consist of three quarks each.
- All matter consists of elementary particles: quarks, electrons and others.
- All elementary particles are "coagulated energy" ($E= mc^2$).
- All energy consists of energy quanta.
- Everything what exists (matter and energy) consists of energy quanta.
- All energy quanta are curvatures of the space-time.
- The space-time is the actually real, which is the basis of everything.

There is from the physical point of view only one something which actually exists: space-time. It is, so to speak, the "substance" of which the whole "tube system" of the superstring theory consists.

This structure of the physical world corresponds thus exactly to the structure of the magic world which leads from the body over the psyche and the soul and then further over the deities to God.

Both views of the world – physical and magical – are a continuum between multiplicity one the one side and unity on the other side.

Due to the tube system model presented in the previous chapter, all structures of the outer world (matter) should be found in the inner world (consciousness) – and also vice versa. This is confirmed by the consideration above: Both the variety of appearances of the material world and the variety of appearances in the world of consciousness can be traced back to a unity underlying this variety: space-time respectively God.

God corresponds thus to space-time – both are the comprehensive One-All-Only, from which multiplicity arises by differentiation.

In this model, life force is (figuratively speaking) the view into the tubes whichdo not belong to one's own body.

One can ask now, of course, what practical use these considerations have.

1. First of all such concepts as the collective subconsciousness become not only more plausible by the tube system model, the collective subconsciousness must exist almost necessarily.

2. The existence of magic is something that should be expected in this model: One can cause an effect by an external movement (normal action) and one can cause an effect by a movement of the consciousness ("will and imagination") (magic action).

3. With the tube system model magical processes can be described quite simply. Whether further experiments or more effective magic methods can be derived from this model is uncertain. In any case, magic appears in this model as expansion, space-grasping and space-occupying, which are quite common terms in connection with magic to begin with.

4. In magic one can distinguish between "ordinary magic" like telepathy and "extraordinary magic" like materializations. Extraordinary magic has a special internal state as a condition, which can be described as "demarcation-lessness".

This state, which appears among others in Buddha's system as the four "boundless states" or on the Kabbalistic Tree of Life as the Sephiroth Da'ath, obviously corresponds to the expansion of consciousness within the tube system: When consciousness has expanded to the entire environment and when individuality no longer needs delimitation for self-definition, but only the certainty of its own quality, then not only ordinary magic is possible, then also "miracles" become possible, i.e. extraordinary magic.

These two types of magic can be described quite simply with the help of the tube system model: In ordinary magic, consciousness expands only a little bit beyond one's own body, while in extraordinary magic it can expand as far as one wants beyond one's own body.

The transition from ordinary magic to extraordinary magic is often experienced in meditation, dream journeys or ritual as a leap into the abyss – one lets go of any hold and any delimitation … which is not quite easy …

5. The gods are in this model so to speak "organizational units" of the consciousness. Thereby either things, which are in analogy to each other, connect to a unit (e.g. the astrological planet Mars), or things, which are only associatively connected (e.g. the mother goddesses).

49

6. The tube system model is a first draft of a comprehensive description of the world, which gives a place to both the physical laws of nature and the magical rules in a unified physical-magical description of the world.

7. The inside and the outside of the tube system, thus consciousness and matter as well as their close connection, are found also in the tradition in many places. The two most concise examples are:

> *"Emptiness is form and form is emptiness."* (Heart Sutra from Buddhism).
> Here emptiness is the underlying unity of consciousness, i.e. "God"; form is the multiplicity of the material world.

> *"Kether is Malkuth and Malkuth is Kether - only in a different way."* (Kabbalah)
> Here, Kether is the unity/God and Malkuth is the multiplicity/world.

The tube system model provides a unified description of the material and magical worlds.

The life force in this model is the perception of the consciousness side of things and beings outside of one's own body, to which one has extended one's consciousness. By this extension of consciousness to other things and beings, the consciousness can perceive these things and beings (telepathy) and move and direct them "as one's own hand" (telekinesis). Therefore, life force is the "substance" and the "power" of magic.

---

13. Fainting, Astral Projection and Trauma

It is worthwhile to take a closer look at some phenomena that at first glance seem to have little to do with the life force, in order to understand the life force even better.

What happens when a person faints? The person loses his consciousness and is therefore "without power" over his body. Obviously, the consciousness has withdrawn from his body. This is, so to speak, the opposite of an expansion of consciousness – and therefore also the opposite of magic.

When one becomes unconscious, one sometimes still has a residue of perception, by which one sees oneself stiffening or falling over, and the like. In addition, it also happens that one sees oneself as if from the outside and also how possibly others take care of one's own body.

Thus, the fainting resembles an astral projection, i.e. the leaving of the material body by the life force body. Also in such an astral projection one sees oneself lying under oneself, while one floats above the material body. However, in astral projection the external circumstances are different – one does not necessarily leave one's own body due to danger, anesthesia, loss of blood, shock or similar, but can also leave it purposefully, e.g. in order to perceive and experience something that is in another place.

So an astral projection is not like a fainting a constriction of the consciousness, by which the consciousness loses control over the body, but rather a shift of consciousness, that is the movement of the consciousness to another place.

If one takes it exactly (which is never completely wrong with a research project), one could also say that the consciousness concentrates during the astral projection completely on the things which are at a certain place outside of one's own body and one experiences oneself therefore in such a way, as if one were also there on the outside. After all, one can concentrate on various things in normal everyday life and completely block out others – why should this not be possible in the realm of consciousness as well?

A faint is like an escape, where you largely limit your entire perception of the world; astral projection is more like an expedition to another place. In magic, one usually expands one's consciousness to another object or being without losing awareness of oneself – though usually everything that does not belong to the instantaneous destination fades into the background.

In the case of trauma, there is another dynamic. A violent experience, which one did not get processed, is in one's own psyche, but is largely isolated from the rest of the psyche.

A trauma arises for example if one is attacked in the steppe from the front by a lion and behind one is a steep ravine. Since one sees no more rescue, the soul gives up and leaves the own body: One detaches the life force body from the material body and makes an astral projection, which from the outside often looks like a fainting – one spares oneself quite simply the experience and the pain of being eaten by the lion.

Now, if other people come and drive the lion away before it has begun its meal, the life force body returns to the material body. As a rule, the person then begins to tremble, scream or cry, whereby the stress of the situation in him dissolves and the life force in him can flow freely again. Then everything is o.k. again.

If, however, such situations are constantly repeated or if the person concerned is unable to dissolve the stress that has arisen in him in this dangerous situation by trembling or the like, the stress remains in the person concerned. This stress has

     1. the intensity of a danger to life,
     2. is connected with the image of the dangerous situation, and is
     3. not accessible, because its dissolution by trembling or the like has been disturbed.

So there is now a stress-laden image in the person concerned that is not readily accessible to him – a panic-filled tin can, so to speak, in the cellar of his own psyche, rattling there on a shelf and spreading fear.

Trauma is therefore a part of the psyche that is no longer integrated with the rest of the psyche.

In astral projection one cannot say for sure that the life-force body or consciousness leaves one's own body, but only that the person concerned concentrates on things outside his body and blocks out his own body – also when a trauma arises, one cannot say for sure whether one is really leaving one's own material body or whether one is only withdrawing one's attention from the physical body in order not to experience being eaten by the lion.

Trauma itself, like powerlessness, is the opposite of magic: not an expansion of consciousness, but a confinement of consciousness – that part of one's psyche which, in the example used here, contains the image of the hungry lion together with the fear of death, is no longer readily accessible.

The healing of such a trauma consists in most cases of a gradual approach to the subject, finding inner and outer support and finally contact with the trauma. Thereby one can open the trauma again, whereupon one once more experiences the whole stress, but does not "get his head under water" and can build up a new image in place of the death anxiety image by the help of (physically present) companions, by gods or the like, in which the death anxiety situation is successfully passed.

The faint and the formation of a trauma are a narrowing of the consciousness. It is possible to experience intense inner processes or even perceptions in the area of consciousness (e.g. seeing the place where one is with closed eyes). These perceptions during a faint are the same as the perceptions during astral projection: Perceptions experienced directly from consciousness without the physical senses. These perceptions are "life force perceptions". They have a different quality – exactly the one of dreams or dream journeys: dimly illuminated, mostly colourless forms in a "foggy" scenery.

Only the initial situation and the circumstances of life are clearly different in the case of a faint and in the case of a voluntary astral projection. A trauma is a faint from which one has not fully returned – the part of the psyche that contains the death fear image is no longer readily accessible to the consciousness, which can be problematic because from then on the person fears everything that has a similarity with this death fear image.

Fainting and trauma are limitations of consciousness and thus the opposite of magic, which is an expansion of consciousness. An astral projection is a shifting of consciousness to the outside of the body.

All perceptions during an astral projection and a faint are life-force perceptions, since they take place without the aid of the physical sense organs – but may well correctly grasp the physical world.

In the case of a trauma, a part of one's own psyche, in which there is a fear-of-death image, becomes largely inaccessible to the conscious mind.

14. Life Force and Precognition

There is one more phenomenon that could make the character of the life force clearer: There is, on the one hand, the possibility of foreseeing things ("precognition") and, on the other hand, the possibility of magically intervening in the shaping of the flow of events from a free impulse of creation. This contradicts itself thoroughly.

If the things are already fixed, it is conceivable to be able to foresee things. If, however, at any time a magician can interfere in the foreseen course of things and change this course, one should not be able to foresee the future. As with most magical phenomena, it is basically only meaningful to talk about such a phenomenon when one has experienced it oneself. If one has foreseen in detail several times events that will not occur for six months, one knows that this possibility exists – otherwise one is dependent on the statements of other people, which can never have the same persuasive power as one's own experience.

Free will and the foreseeing of events are a contradiction. Contradictions, which however exist in reality, are an indication that one sees only two fragments of the world and not yet the total context.

Within this contradiction also the life force plays a role, because in it the imaginations are created by the free will, which then intervene by their magic effect in the causally determined course of the events and reshape them.

Are there several possible forms of the future? But then, why can one still foresee the future?

Or then, if someone has foreseen the future, can't a magician interfere with the course of foreseen things? That would be an amazingly-man-centered dynamic …

Does foreseeing an event make that event "fixed"? Does the foreseeing of an event thus correspond to the creation of an event by "will and imagination"? The foreseeing and the magical creating are both "life force images" …

The exact connection between precognition and the possibility of free imprinting of events by magic remains uncertain for the time being – first of all, these two possibilities form a contradiction: If the future is fixed, one cannot change anything in the course of events on the way to this future – which, however, is exactly what one is able to do due to magic.

---

15. Self-Organization of the Life Force

Now that many phenomena of the life force have been considered, the question arises whether there is such a thing as a "self-organization of the life force" – just as atoms combine to form molecules, molecules combine to form cells, cells combine to form organs, organs combine to form living beings, living beings combine to form communities, and so on.

In order to be able to find this out, it is helpful to consider first of all all known inherent dynamics of the life force. In the following, the phenomena already considered as well as some further observations are listed.

1. Perception of life force

- The life force can be perceived in a direct way as an "electric tingle" or as a milky-white, luminous mist with a slight blue glow – on people, animals, plants, electrical appliances, etc.
- The life force is experienced in dreams and dream journeys as mostly fuzzy colorless shapes in a space filled with a diffuse light that has no source, but is rather a "translucent, luminous mist."
- The life force is directed in magic and in some forms of healing by will and imagination, that is, by consciousness.
- The life force appears as light, warmth, tactile sensation, and the like, that is, always as a sensation corresponding to material perceptions. However, these sensations are easily distinguishable from physical sensations with some practice – the heat of Kundalini, for example, is clearly different from the heat of a hearth or the heat of the sun, even though both are heat.

=> The life force is perceptible in the forms of physical sensations (light, heat, touch, etc.), but is still distinctly different from physical sensations. There is no independent life force perception that is as clearly different from physical perceptions as seeing is different from hearing. So there is a connection between the life force and the physical senses.

The life force seems to be in everything (perception as a luminous mist) and also to fill all space (diffuse light in dreams).

2. Basic phenomena

- Telepathy shows that the life force can extend from the consciousness of one person to the consciousness of another person, animal, place or object.
- Telekinesis shows that by this expansion of consciousness, which is experienced as an expansion of life force, one cannot only perceive, but also act.

> => The life force is at the same time "eye" (telepathy) and "hand" (telekinesis). The life force is experienced as an expansion of one's own consciousness, which is equivalent to an expansion of one's own life force – thereby other people, animals, plants, and objects temporarily become a part of one's own body: by expanding one's own consciousness, one expands the access area of one's own consciousness, i.e. one grasps and occupies things outside of one's own body and temporarily makes them a part of one's own body. Thus one can perceive in them as in one's own body and act with them as with one's own body, i.e. move them e.g. "by telekinesis".
>
> The life force and thus also telepathy and telekinesis are closely coupled to matter as well as to consciousness. One can regard the life force consequently as the border area between consciousness and matter.

3. Special phenomena

- Most mothers (and some fathers) can sense how their children are doing – especially when the children are still very small. For example, they can sense when the children are in danger and intuitively look what the children are doing. This "standard telepathic connection" between mother and child can be perceived as an "umbilical cord" of milky white light, that is, a life force umbilical cord. It leads from the solar plexus of the mother to the solar plexus of the child.
- Such umbilical cords are apparently also formed by emotional bonds, friendships, meditating together, working together for long periods of time, etc., and especially by sexuality, as they are found primarily between relationship partners (or are at least most noticeable there). Through these life force umbilical cords, also called "silver cords", inner images, moods and the like flow from one person to the other. Even such things as beer addiction can be transmitted through these umbilical cords. (I once experienced this myself as a violent thirst for beer, although I never drink alcohol.) It is likely that this type of life force exchange, including the semi-conscious telepathy associated with it, occurs much more often than is actually noticed.

The beer thirst example shows that the information transmitted telepathically "via silver cord" can be very precise, but it is possible to be even more detailed: I once advised a friend and colleague about 20 years ago and suddenly had the very strong urge to take off my shirt and undershirt. I found that rather strange, but the inner urge was so strong that I did it. Only much later I learned from her that she had been abused as a child for several years and that the taking off of his shirt by the man had always been the beginning of the catastrophe – she had not been able to heal this abuse trauma at that time and it was also in the air in our encounters, since I was clearly older than her (as was the man who had abused her as a child).

- A special form of telepathy is dominant people who immediately fill a room when they enter it or in whose presence you can no longer think independently. They extend their consciousness and imprinting to their entire surrounding space. I know a magician who imprints his surrounding space within a radius of 15m – i.e. the area of his surrounding space that can be seen from him.

- There is a phenomenon which another magician has given the nice name "Nega-Psi", i.e. "negative Psi". This word discribes the effect that people in the closer environment of a certain person (e.g. the 15m in the case of said magician) are unable to perform telepathy or telekinesis and in extreme cases are even unable to perform their handicraft. This is sometimes quite troublesome for these "dominance mages" …

- A variant of the last example are PCs that break down due to the stress of their user. Here, too, one can partly observe a radius of action with a sharp border. In the case of an acquaintance of mine this is 4m – if she is in stress and e.g. wants to visit someone in the hospital, she has to step back 4m from the reception desk, so that their PC starts again.

- Astral projection is a special case of telepathy, where the consciousness is extended to the environment in a much clearer way than in telepathy. This has the effect that one experiences oneself with one's consciousness and with one's ability to perceive in another place, i.e. as outside of one's own body. Astral projection also occurs during fainting. Both of these are also part of the dynamics in the occurrence of trauma – where the consciousness (astral body) abandons its own physical body and leaves it temporarily.

- Finally, there is "life force vampirism," in which life force is intentionally or unintentionally drained from another person. The effect of this is that the "vampire" becomes stronger and stronger, more alert and energetic, while his victim becomes weaker and weaker and eventually falls asleep. Such processes are also found in many relationships or between superior and subordinate. The shifting of life force takes place e.g. also in every quarrel – there the commitment of the two parties involved determines how much life force they put on the line … and the winner gets all the life force and therefore feels good and alive, while the loser feels weak.

Presumably "getting life force" in the mentioned cases is identical with "getting control over a life force area", i.e. over a subject, a part of a person and the like.

=> There are fixed telepathic connections: the life force umbilical cords. They are found between people who have a close bond – especially between mother and child. Through such "silver cords" the most different informations, qualities, impulses etc. can flow from one human being to another – unconsciously, half-consciously and partly also consciously (in magic). Life force also flows from one person to another through these silver cords, causing weakening and strengthening.

The attitude of the "sender" of such information is sometimes extremely dominant – he then takes over the whole room and shapes it, directing the events in this room and partly also the actions of the people in this room. Such a person can also block the abilities of the people around him ("Nega-Psi").

The constant expansion of consciousness to the surrounding space, i.e. the expansion of one's own life force body can have a clearly recognizable limit from which the influence and imprint of this person ceases.

Astral projections and faints are in a way an extreme form of telepathy, since in them the consciousness and thus the point from which the environment is perceived is outside the physical body (sometimes in a distant place).

4. Systematic use of the life force

- The possibilities of telepathy, which lie in the life force, are systematically used in family constellations. It is shown that for this form of telepathy no special talent and also no special training is necessary. Moreover, family constellations show that even complex situations can be precisely grasped by a group of people in a telepathic way.
- In Reiki, diseases are healed with the help of the life force.
- With the help of the life force, machines can also be "healed", i.e. repaired.
- In mesmerism ("animal magnetism"), diseases are cured by directing the life force, or people are put under hypnosis by influencing their life force bodies.
- In homeopathy, too, the life force in the globules works, not the material substance of the globules.
- Many forms of meditation consist of directing the life force in the body – e.g. as kundalini in the chakras. This also has a healing effect.
- In acupuncture and acupressure, the body is also healed by influencing the life force – even if this is not so obvious here.
- In Karate and similar martial arts the life force is used to strengthen the body.
- Probably also demagogues use intuitively the directing of the life force – however, this cannot be proved with certainty.
- In hypnosis, the hypnotist extends his consciousness to the hypnotized person and can then direct him like his own body. This becomes very clear especially in remote

hypnosis ("telepathic hypnosis").

- In magic there is the approach that the magician grasps, shapes and directs his surrounding space, the conversations and the persons in his surrounding space with his consciousness. This is a more comprehensive and intense form of hypnosis.

- In magic, chance is directed with the help of will and imagination, that is, with the help of the expansion of one's consciousness.

- In magic, information can be stored in objects – for example, by consecrating a talisman.

> => The life force can contain complex structures and apparently take large, organic forms.

> These complex forms can be in their natural state and thus healthy or they can be disturbed and thus diseased. Diseases (and even disturbances of machines) can be also healed by the life force.

> Life force imprinted with information can be stored in objects (talismans, globules, etc.).

> Life force can strengthen physical power (Karate).

> In hypnosis and magic one's own consciousness is extended to another person – this is so to say "invasive telepathy".

> By the extension of the consciousness by "will and imagination" also coincidences can be directed.

5. The temporal self-organization of the life force

- Since the life force is the "substance" of the psyche, possibly also the memory belongs to the characteristics of the life force – even if memory can be explained with the electro-chemical storage of information in the brain.

- The telepathic memory of events long time ago (which can be verified afterwards) is a form of information acquisition which cannot be traced back to an electro-chemical storage of information. However, one cannot say with certainty whether this is "time telepathy" into the past or a recognition e.g. of the archaeological findings, with which one can confirm these perceptions afterwards.

- However, the proof of "time telepathy" is possible with the help of homeopathy: the remedies partly act according to the past history of the substance from which the remedy is made. For example, Lycopodium (Lycopodium) is effective in a certain form of depression, in which one believes that one is only living in the movie credits and that one's great time is already over. Today Lycopodium is a small herb at the edge of the forest – 300 million years ago most of the plants on earth consisted of Lycopodium plants. They gave rise to coal, lignite, oil and natural gas – today's

Lycopodium lives on the mass graves of its ancestors …

So Lycopodium has a memory that goes back 300 million years and is not based on electro-chemical storage of information: time telepathy.

- One can also interpret reincarnation as time telepathy: The events of a person's life in earlier times can be linked time-telepathically to the consciousness of a present-day person.

- Foreseeing the future shows that there is also a time telepathy into the future.

- The same is also proved by astrology: It is possible to say already today what character a person will have who will be born in the year 2137 A.D. at 5.35PM in Berlin.

> => Telepathy arranges the contents of the life force not only in spatial terms, but also in temporal terms: there is spatial telepathy and temporal telepathy. The "temporal distance" can be very big and in some cases it includes 300 million years.
>
> This time telepathy reaches into the past as well as into the future.
>
> Since in physics space and time are firmly connected to space-time, it is actually not surprising that also in telepathy a spatial and a temporal extension of consciousness is possible.

6. The change of the inner images

- The inner images of the psyche, i.e. imprinting of the individual life force, can be changed and healed by magic, meditations, trauma healing, family constellations, etc.

> => The imprinting of the life force is not a permanent imprinting, but a temporary imprinting. However, earlier imprints are still accessible by time telepathy.

7. Forms of inner perception

- The life force is perceived in different ways depending on the type of consciousness. The different types of consciousness may therefore show different "layers" of the life force, i.e. different steps/stages/areas at the boundary between consciousness and matter.

> - Ecstasy consciousness is entirely on the "matter side." During a state of lust, fear, pain, meditation and the like, exclusively one single content of consciousness is perceived – this cannot be more concrete and specific. Here the external perception dominates.

- The waking consciousness is also still on the "matter side", but here already all perceptions, which are of importance in the momentary situation, are combined and processed. Here, too, the external perception dominates.

- In the dream-consciousness (subconsciousness) all contents of consciousness are equally present. They are usually perceived as slightly diffuse and largely colorless images that are in a misty light that has no definite source. Here the life force itself appears for the first time as a nebulous light.

- In deep sleep and in deep meditation or in intense dream journeys, one is in the realm of the soul and individuality, i.e. on the middle area between consciousness and matter. Here you can find mainly symbols and figures, that shine from within, are colored, and are usually unmoving pictures – they are the essences, which shape one's own being. Here, the life force is already clearly more intense: the colorful glow of the symbols and figures from within.

- In the area of consciousness corresponding to the gods, contours are perceived in the light (e.g. gods). Here the light dominates, i.e. the life force, which is only little structured by contents. Here the light is a continuum.

- In the realm of oneness (the One God, space-time) only a glistening white light or a shining blackness is perceived. Here there is only the One-All-Only, but no more differentiation.

- On the transition from matter to consciousness the perceptions become more and more abstract and less and less concrete. On the matter side the life force consists of sharply delimited units – on the consciousness side there is only the all-embracing unity. In between there are the levels of the dream, the soul and the gods. One could describe this transition approximately as follows:

- matter =   4/4 matter + 0/4 consciousness
- dream =   3/4 matter + 1/4 consciousness
- soul =   2/4 matter + 2/4 consciousness
- deities =   1/4 matter + 3/4 consciousness
- God =   0/4 matter + 4/4 consciousness

- The main property of matter is its determinacy – the main property of consciousness is its freedom. From this it follows that the area between these two poles is creativity, i.e. the area in which magic and also astrology take place.

=> The border area between consciousness and matter is perceived as life force. This border area is not a sharp, narrow line, but an area that can be divided into several levels, which on the matter side consists of individual, delimited units and on the consciousness side consists of an all-encompassing unity. In the middle between both stands the "unit size" of the soul.

8. General structures of the inner images

- Astrology shows that the realm of life force is ordered by analogies: the character of a person is described by the planetary position at the time of his birth (horoscope). The same principle of analogy is also found in homeopathy and magic, among others. The principle of analogy says that like acts on like, that like develops alike, that like attaches to like, etc. By these analogies, the all-encompassing unity on the consciousness side of the life force gradually develops from the individual elements on the matter side of the life force.

=> The gradual transition between multiplicity and unity in the realm of the life force is ordered by analogies.

9. The "geometry" of the life force

- The life force contains some basic structures which are, so to speak, analogy essences, i.e. analogy structures which can be found everywhere. These are seven different principles. They are only briefly outlined here – a more detailed description of their properties may be found in my book "Number Symbolism for Beginners". These seven principles are:
- The "1" is the principle of unity and therefore of identity. The "1" is unipolar and therefore corresponds to gravitation, which exists only in a single form, which affects everything. In astrology the "1" is the conjunction.
- The "2" is the principle of the complementary opposition, which causes a constant movement. It corresponds to the electromagnetic force, which has the two poles "+" and "–" or "north" and "south". It appears further as Yin and Yang and also as man and woman. The dynamics of the "2" is described in detail and very differentiated in the I Ching. The relationship mandala is also an application of this dynamic (see "Mandalas for Beginners"). In astrology, the "2" is the opposition.
- The "3" is a three-polarity and a three-step, which appears in physics, among other things, as the three-polar color force, which can have the qualities "red", "yellow" and "blue". They form a solid cohesion. In astrology, the three steps are the three dynamics of the zodiac signs, that is, "cardinal", "fixed" and "mobile". They appear in the chakras as the three pairs of chakras by which the identity in the heart chakra becomes concrete: unhindered self-expression (solar plexus and throat chakra) – creation of forms (hara and third eye) – contact (root chakra and crown chakra). The most differentiated system based on the dynamics of the "3" is the Kabbalistic Tree of Life. In astrology,

the "3" is the trine.

- The "4" is a "double 2": two complementary oppositions form a cross together – like the electric wave and the magnetic wave in a photon. The "4" spans a space. In astrology the "4" is the square.

- The "5" is the principle of transformation – it corresponds to the weak interaction, which causes among other things that atomic nuclei can decay and transform. In astrology the "5" is the quincunx.

- The "6" is the principle of the formation of groups from equal elements. The "6" is found as a 60° angle in honeycombs, in snow crystals, in the arrangement of moons in the same orbit, in the electron shell, in the arrangement of protons and neutrons in atomic nuclei, and much more. In astrology, the "6" is the sextile.

- The "12" is the combination of the numbers "1" to "6". It is therefore the number of the basic units in our world: on the matter side the structure of the superstring as a twelve-divided circle and on the magic side the structure of the Zodiac as a twelve-divided circle. In astrology the "12" is the half-sextile.

- These analogy essences are all found both in matter and in the realm of life force (consciousness, magic, astrology). This is simply because the life force realm connects to matter on one of its two sides and consequently must have the same structures as matter. The more concrete forms of the life-force consist of the life-force bodies of men, animals, plants, stones, etc. The more general analogies, by which the life-force is combined into ever larger units up to the all-embracing unity, consists of the seven structures which have just been briefly described: "1", "2", "3", "4", "5", "6" and "12".

=> The analogies are based in their core on the dynamics of the six numbers "1", "2", "3", "4", "5" and "6" which are summarized in the "12". The "12" is the basic form of matter (superstrings) and consciousness (zodiac).

10. The power of inner images

- First of all, telepathy and telekinesis show that the life force and the images imprinted in it can be extremely effective – one can find lost objects with them or repair a cordless screwdriver … and with their help one can, among other things, break bricks with karate …

- Another example of the great effect of the life force and the images and structures in it is the horoscope, which describes the character of a person. The repetition compulsion that is well known from psychology is also partly based on this "astrological imprinting".

There is no possibility to leave one's own horoscope, but one can live it on a higher and higher level, so that the horoscope is not a "prison", but rather the theme for the symphony of one's own life, which one composes.

- One's own freedom of decision, which is in man originating from the side of consciousness, makes it possible, by striving for creativity and self-determination, to act less and less inwardly and outwardly compulsively, but instead to become freer and freer, and thus also to exercise more and more effective magic.

> => As astrology, magic, homeopathy, karate, etc. show, the images contained in the life force are extremely effective. Increasing awareness of these images and striving for autonomy makes it possible to use and create these images in a targeted way and thus to be able to perform effective magic.

11. The inner world of images

- The images in one's own psyche, that is, one's own inner imagery, is telepathically connected to the images in other people. The images in one's own psyche are also, as astrology shows, connected to the planets that shape a person's character (horoscope) and the variation of that character at any given moment (transits).
- The images in different people are connected to each other to form archetypes – they are the most important contents of the collective subconsciousness.
- The relationship mandala shows, among other things, the way in which people's inner images give rise to image-couplings, i.e. "communities": In the very simplest approach, the independent seeks the independent, the addict and the ascetic seek each other, the perpetrator and the victim seek each other, and the star and the fan seek each other; in the most complex approach, the relationship between two people is shaped by the relationship of the planets in the chart of one to the planets in the chart of the other.
- Presumably this image-coupling applies not only to humans, but also to animals, plants, etc., since they too contain life force and therefore consciousness and a horoscope as well as inner images. This general image-coupling probably creates an overall structure of life force of the earth – it is sometimes called "Gaia".
- A person's connection to the collective subconsciousness is probably identical with the Kundalini, which is the life force of the Earth. It rises from the Earth's core, which is the root chakra of the Earth, into a person's root chakra as if through a life force umbilical cord, and then causes the upward flow of the life force in the person.

> => The images in the life force of individual beings combine to the form archetypes – and these then ultimately form the collective consciousnessness of the earth.

12. The use of the collective subconsciousness

- The best known use of the collective subconscious is telepathy, which form the connections between the individual elements of the collective subconscious, i.e. the images in the psyches of people. The same is true for telekinesis and consequently for magic as a whole.
- Another form of use is self-healing by the connection to the primal images, i.e. mainly to the deities.
- A still little used possibility is the coordination within an economic system by telepathy, i.e. by the collective subconsciousness. Summoning needed things, relationships, friendships, apartments, jobs, etc. by magic is a first beginning of this economic form, in which the wishing brings about what is needed and in which one sends out into the world what one wants to give oneself. I have described this economic form in my books "Money Magic for Beginners" and "Von innerer Fülle zu äußerem Wohlstand". This form of economic activity is so far mainly used by magicians and in "sects" whose members firmly trust in a deity (Christ, Krishna, Shiva, etc.).

> => The collective subconsciousness is due to its character (archetypes and telepathy) suitable to take over coordination tasks. This is possible if one trusts this collective subconsciousness or trusts simply the gods (archetypes) in it. The economic form corresponding to this is so far used only by individuals and by small groups.

Summary 1

Through the reflections on the self-organization of the life force in this book, the following points have become clear:

> - The life force is perceived primarily as light-mist and as heat (clairvoyance, Kundalini).

> - The life force is the transitional area between matter and consciousness – it is shaped by the forms of matter and by the contents of consciousness. The life force is both perceiving (telepathy) and acting (telekinesis) – there is no difference between both in the life force.

> - Everything is matter and in everything is consciousness – consequently in everything is also the transition between consciousness and matter, i.e. in everything there is the life force area or more exactly the life force transition between matter and consciousness. Therefore everything can be grasped by

telepathy and everything can be influenced by telekinesis. Since matter is organized in a complex way, the life force is also organized in complex structures. These forms can be healthy (undisturbed) or sick (disturbed) – and they can be healed or repaired on the level of life force.

- Life force connections between two people can be perceived as life force umbilical cords. These life force umbilical cords are also used in magic e.g. in consecrations and in remote hypnosis. The complex structures that are perceived by a group of people during a family constellation, for example, consist of a web of such life force umbilical cords.

The consciousness of a person, i.e. his life force body can also be extended to complex situations, which are then controlled by the magician. This area consciously controlled by the magician (remote hypnosis, dominance) and also the area unconsciously shaped by a person (PC crash) can have a very clear boundary (e.g. the radius of 4m). By the intentional expansion of the consciousness by "will and imagination" also coincidences can be directed.

Taking control over another (hypnosis), victory over another and also direct life force vampirism give the dominant person additional life force that is under their control, i.e. the dominant person gains control over another person, over a topic, over an affair, etc. As a result, these dominant people become stronger and stronger.

- During astral travel, consciousness as the "point from which one perceives" is transferred out of the body to any place.

- Life force imprinted with information can be stored in objects (talismans, homeopathic globules, etc.).

The imprinting of life force is not a permanent imprinting, but a temporary imprinting.

- Life force can strengthen physical power (karate, etc.).

- Life force is not as isolated as matter, but rather a continuum similar to a force field – this is evident in telepathy and telekinesis. Since there are many forms of conscious use of the life force (hypnosis, consecration, magic, etc.) and also quite a few forms of semi-conscious use (life force umbilical cord between mother and child, etc.) and also unconscious effects (astrology), it can be assumed that there is a great deal of unconscious telepathic exchange between people, i.e. a complex network of permanent or even short-term connections in the form of life force umbilical cords. This largely unconscious network is the collective subconscious.

- Telepathy orders the contents of the life force not only in spatial terms, but also in temporal terms: there is spatial telepathy and temporal telepathy. This temporal telepathy reaches both back into the past and ahead into the future. The spatial-temporal telepathy corresponds to the space-time as the basis of physics.

- The border area between consciousness and matter is perceived as life force. This border area is not a sharp, narrow line, but an area which can be divided into several levels, which consists on the matter side of single, delimited units and on the consciousness side of an all-embracing unit. In the middle between both stands the "unit size" of the soul.

The gradual transition between multiplicity and unity in the realm of the life force is ordered by analogies.

- The analogies are based in their core on the dynamics of the six numbers "1", "2", "3", "4", "5" and "6", which are summarized in the "12", which is the basic form of matter (superstrings) and consciousness (zodiac).

- As astrology, magic, homeopathy, karate, etc. show, the images contained in the life force are extremely effective. Increasing awareness of these images and striving for autonomy makes it possible to use and create these images in a purposeful way and thus to be able to perform effective magic.

- The images in the life force of the individual beings combine to form archetypes – and these then ultimately form an overall consciousness of the earth.

The collective subconsciousness is because of its character (archetypes and telepathy) suitable to take over coordination tasks. This is possible if one trusts this collective subconsciousness or simply trusts the gods (archetypes). The economic form corresponding to this is so far used only by individuals and by small groups.

Summary 2

One can present the points of "Summary 1" once again in a shorter, concise form in order to be able to grasp the self-organization of the life force as clearly as possible:

- The life force is perceived as light-mist and as heat.

- The life force is the transition area between matter and consciousness. Everything is matter and in everything is consciousness. Consequently, there is also life force in everything, i.e. a transition between matter and consciousness.

- The life force is both perceiving (telepathy) and acting (telekinesis).

- The contents of the consciousness and consequently the life force are as complex or as simple as the structure of the matter of which this consciousness is the inside.

- The images in the consciousness can be changed – this enables among other things also healings by life force.

- Life force connections can be perceived as life force umbilical cords – they can be permanent or temporary. They form complex networks in groups of people, living beings and things. This network is the collective subconsciousness of humans, the collective subconsciousness of an animal species, the collective subconsciousness of a plant species, etc. which together eventually form the collective subconsciousness of the Earth ("Gaia").

- The permanent area of influence of the life force body of a human being has a clear outer limit, which is between 0m (unprotected) and about 15m (dominant) – mostly about 70cm. Magic is essentially the expansion of the area in which the magician's consciousness takes control of people and things.

- In astral projection, consciousness as the "point from which one perceives" is moved out of the body to any place.

- Life force imprinted with information can be stored in objects (talismans, homeopathic globules, etc.).

- Life force can strengthen the body power.

- Telepathy arranges the contents of life force both in space and time. This also enables telepathic perception of the past and the future.

- The boundary area between consciousness and matter is not a sharp, narrow line, but an area that can be divided into several stages, which on the matter side consists of individual, delimited units and on the consciousness side of an all-encompassing unity. In the middle between both stands the "unit size" of the soul.

The gradual transition between multiplicity and unity in the realm of the life force is ordered by analogies.

The analogies are based in their core on the dynamics of the six numbers "1", "2", "3", "4", "5" and "6", which are summarized in the "12", which is the basic form of matter (superstrings) and consciousness (zodiac).

- The collective subconsciousness, because of its character (primordial images and telepathy), is suitable to take over coordination tasks. This is possible if one trusts this collective subconsciousness or simply trusts the gods (archetypes). The economic form corresponding to this is so far used only by individuals and by small groups.

Summary 3

Finally, one can summarize these results once again in a bullet point manner:

- life force = light-mist and heat

- life force = telepathy + telekinesis
- life force can enhance physical strength

- life force = spatial and temporal connections
- life force connections = life force umbilical cords
- life force connections form complex networks whose essences are the archetypes (gods)

- life force images are in principle changeable, but can also remain the same for a longer time (storage facility)
- images of the life force = depend on the complexity of the material basis

- the range of influence of a human life force body is usually around 70cm; it can be between 0m and 15m
- astral projection = comprehensive telepathy, in which the entire perceptive ability is transferred to a point outside of the body

- life force = border area between consciousness and matter = gradual transition from delimited units to an all-encompassing unity
- life force is structured by analogies ("1", "2", "3", "4", "5", "6", "12")
- structural basic element of life force: 12-part circle (superstring, zodiac)

- the collective subconsciousbess is able to coordinate: astrology, magic, economic system

Summary 4

Now a final summary of the self-organization of the life force is possible:

The life force is the transition between consciousness and matter with its own spatio-temporal structure and dynamics (analogies, "12"), consisting of a network of spatial and temporal connections.

The life force forms from its matter side to its consciousness side more and more comprehensive units – from the psyche (life force body of a human being) to the all-encompassing consciousness (God).

Diagram

Possibly these results become a little more tangible as a diagram. The basic structure of this diagram is the life force as the perception of the transition between consciousness and matter.

Self-organization of the life force						
Matter	*Life force*					*Consciousness*
outside	identity					inside
multiplicity	organic forms					unity
determinacy	creativity					freedom
spatio-temporal effects	spatio-temporal connections					being
matter	total organization as collective subconsciousness					consciousness
matter	body	psyche	soul	protec-tive deity	"enligh-tened state	god
matter	images of matter	dream images	identity images	deity Images	unity-image	consciousness
matter in itself	external percep-tion	diffuse, mostly colorless images	symbols shining from within	contours in the light	undifferen-tiated, glistening white light	consciousness itself
causality	analogies (astrology, tree of life, I Ching, numbers etc.)					freedom
causal effects	telepathy, telekinesis					freedom of unity
causal effects	magic: "guidance of chance" and "non-causal effects					freedom

70

16. Summary

The life force is not a magical substance that exists in addition to normal matter. Instead, it is a name for a special form of perception and action that emanates from consciousness and takes place in the realm of consciousness. This way of perceiving and acting is usually called "magic".

The life force is a descriptive model for the non-physical, i.e. magical, connections that can be demonstrated by telepathy, telekinesis, homeopathy, astrology, and the like.

The life force can be directed by humans and possibly also others creatures. It can transmit information as well as effects. It can also be sent (telepathy) and stored (consecrations). The life force, at least of humans, is structured and organized (chakras, kundalini) and can temporarily leave the physical body (astral projection), in which case the consciousness and the ability to perceive is bound to the life force body and not to the physical body.

The life force is closely connected with consciousness and can therefore also appear as astral bodies, spirits, gods and the like. The life force part of a human being is his life force body (astral body) which corresponds to his psyche in its contents.

The life force has no own form of perception, but is perceived in the forms of the physical senses as image, sound, touch, heat etc.. The life force can also be perceived "object-free" as light – possibly the inner "silence" well known from meditation also corresponds to this.

The life force organizes itself in a polar-symmetrical structure. These structure elements of the life force are in the human being above all the seven main chakras ("life force organs"), which are connected with each other by a convection current ("life force circuit"). A part of this circuit is the Kundalini. The same structure is found in the structure of a star. As a symbol, this structure appears as a vajra.

The very detailed correspondence of the structures in the realm of the life force and in the realm of matter shows that the life force is an "inner perception of the world". The life force is the description of the world as it looks when seen from the consciousness – when one inwardly extends one's own consciousness to another being or thing and then perceives it and, if necessary, can direct it like one's own arm.

Imagination is the creation of an inner image, which then receives an impulse by the will.

Will is an inner freedom whose root is ultimately God's freedom – or, more abstractly, whose root is ultimately the unity of consciousness underlying all indicidual consciousnesses.

Imagination is the counterpart to perception: In perception, one sees something in one's consciousness that is already there on the outside – in imagination, one creates an image in one's consciousness that then becomes reality on the outside.

The analogies are a structure, which is found in the area of the consciousness and secondarily also in the physical world. These analogies should be taken into account in magic in order to take the easiest way to one's goal. The essences of this structure are the six numbers "1", "2", "3", "4", "5" and "6", which are summarized in the "12", which is the basic form of matter (superstrings) and consciousness (zodiac).

The life force forms from its matter side to its consciousness side more and more comprehensive units – from the psyche (life force body of a human being) to the all-encompassing consciousness (God).

The life force appears at the border between the determinacy of the material world and the freedom of the consciousness. However, life force is not an independent substance, but the direct perception of the consciousness in the realm of the consciousness – it is the transition between matter and consciousness with its own spatio-temporal structure and dynamics (analogies, "12"), consisting of a network of spatial and temporal connections.

The tube system model originating from the superstring theory allows a unified description of the material and the magical world.

The life force in this model is the perception of the consciousness side of things outside of one's own body, to which one has extended one's consciousness. By this extension of consciousness to other things and beings, consciousness can move and direct these things and beings "as one's own hand". Therefore, the life force is the "substance" and the "power" of magic.

Matter is the outside of the world – consciousness is the inside of the world – life force is the transition between both.

Life force is what you perceive when you extend your consciousness beyond your own body and perceive other things and beings from the inside, that is, from consciousness.

The concept of life force is widespread throughout the world. There are no traditional ideas about different types of life force, but only about different manifestations of life force. The life force sustains life, is closely related to "rightness" and is perceived primarily as light or heat.

The life force is a self-evident concept in the myths, but it is personified to a deity only in a few cases and then only in the late phases of a mythology.

English Books by Harry Eilenstein

- Living Magic (261 p.)
- The Synthesis of Physics and Magic (192 p.)
- Telepathy for Beginners (60 p.)
- Telepathy for Advanced Learners (52 p.)
- Telekinesis for Beginners (56 p.)
- Life Force for Beginners (76 p.)
- Astral Projection for Beginners (60 p.)
- Meditation for Beginners (60 p.)
- Prophecy for Beginners (60 p.)
- Invocations for Beginners (52 p.)
- Evocations for Beginners (62 p.)
- Auto-Movement for Beginners (60 p.)
- Elves for Beginners (56 p.)
- Hypnosis for Beginners (56 p.)
- Love Magic for Beginners (52 p.)
- Money Magic for Beginners (60 p.)
- Magic Objects for Beginners (64 p.)
- Shamanism for Beginners (52 p.)
- Self Knowledge for Beginners (60 p.)

- Number Symbolism for Beginners (64 p.)
- Ritual Magic for Beginners (64 p.)
- Mandalas for Beginners (76 p.)
- Crop Circles for Beginners (344 p.)
- Feng Shui for Beginners (96 p.)

These books will be puplished soon:

- Kundalini for Beginners
- Chakra-Magic for Beginners
- Astrology for Beginners
- Magic Research for Beginners
- Symbolism of Numbers for Beginners
- Language of the Moon – for Beginners
- Magic Chant for Beginners
- Da'ath-Magic for Beginners
- Magic for Beginners – Anthology I
- Magic for Beginners – Anthology II
- Magic for Beginners – Anthology III
- Magic for Beginners – Anthology IV

Bücher von Harry Eilenstein

Religion allgemein
- Die sieben Schritte des Lebens (428 S.)
- Muttergöttin und Schamanen (168 S.)
- Göbekli Tepe (472 S.)
- Die Göttin von Göbekli Tepe (144 S.)
- Totempfähle (440 S.)
- Christus (60 S.)
- Dakini (80 S.)
- Vajra (76 S.)

Ägypten
- Hathor und Re 1: Götter und Mythen im Alten Ägypten (432 S.)
- Hathor und Re 2: Die altägyptische Religion – Ursprünge, Kult und Magie (396 S.)
- Isis (508 S.)

Indogermanen
- Die Entwicklung der indogermanischen Religionen (700 S.)
- Wurzeln und Zweige der indogermanischen Religion (224 S.)

Germanen
- Die Götter der Germanen (87 Bände – siehe nächste Seite)
- Odin (300 S.)

Kelten
- Cernunnos (690 S.)
- Taliesin (228 S.)
- Der Kessel von Gundestrup (220 S.)
- Der Chiemsee-Kessel (76)

Psychologie
- Über die Freude (100 S.)
- Das Geheimnis des inneren Friedens (252 S.)
- Das Beziehungsmandala (52 S.)
- Gefühle und ihre Verwandlungen (404 S.)
- einsgerichtet (140 S.)
- Liebe und Eigenständigkeit (216 S.)
- Von innerer Fülle zu äußerem Gedeihen (52 S.)

Heilung
- Die Symbolik der Krankheiten (76 S.)

Kunst
- Herz des Tanzes – Tanz des Herzens (160 S.)

Drama
- König Athelstan (104 S.)

Bücher von Harry Eilenstein

„Magie für Anfänger"

- Telepathie für Anfänger (60 S.)
- Telepathie für Fortgeschrittene (52 S.)
- Telekinese für Anfänger (52 S.)
- Lebenskraft für Anfänger (60 S.)
- Meditation für Anfänger (56 S.)
- Kundalini für Anfänger (100 S.)
- Hypnose für Anfänger (56 S.)
- Auto-Movement für Anfänger (56 S.)
- Chakra-Magie für Anfänger (148 S.)
- Astralreisen für Anfänger (56 S.)
- Astrologie für Anfänger (120 S.)
- Ritual-Magie für Anfänger (56 S.)
- Mandalas für Anfänger (68 S.)
- Geldzauber für Anfänger (56 S.)
- Liebeszauber für Anfänger (52 S.)
- Invokationen für Anfänger (52 S.)
- Evokationen für Anfänger (60 S.)
- Elfen für Anfänger (56 S.)
- Magie-Forschung für Anfänger (140 S.)
- Selbsterkenntnis für Anfänger (52 S.)
- Zahlensymbolik für Anfänger (60 S.)
- Die Sprache des Mondes – für Anfänger (116 S.)
- Zaubergesänge für Anfänger (100 S.)
- Zukunftschau für Anfänger (60 S.)
- Schamanismus für Anfänger (52 S.)
- Magische Gegenstände für Anfänger (68 S.)
- Da'ath-Magie für Anfänger (64 S.)
- Kornkreise für Anfänger (348 S.)
- Feng Shui für Anfänger (96 S.)
- Magie für Anfänger – Sammelband I (696 S.)
- Magie für Anfänger – Sammelband II (664 S.)
- Magie für Anfänger – Sammelband III (580 S.)

„Traumreisen"

- Traumreisen zu Heilpflanzen (700 S.)

Magie

- Handbuch für Zauberlehrlinge (408 S.)
- Tarot (104 S.)
- Physik und Magie (184 S.)
- Die Synthese von Physik und Magie (200S.)
- Die Magie-Formel (156 S.)
- Krafttiere – Tiergöttinnen – Tiertänze (112 S.)
- Schwitzhütten (524 S.)
- Mythen und Magie der Harfe (116 S.)
- Magie heute – Berichte aus der Praxis (288 S.)

Meditation

- Der Lebenskraftkörper (230 S.)
- Die Chakren (100 S.)
- Das Chakren-System mit den Nebenchakren (296 S.)
- Organe und Chakren (64 S.)
- Die platonischen Körper in den Chakren (156 S.)
- Meditation (140 S.)
- Drachenfeuer (124 S.)
- Kundalini I (676 S.)
- Reinkarnation (156 S.)
- einsgerichtet (140 S.)

Astrologie

- Astrologie (496 S.)
- Photo-Astrologie (428 S.)
- Die astrologischen Aspekte (88 S.)
- Horoskop und Seele (120 S.)

Kabbala

- Kursus der praktischen Kabbala (150 S.)
- Eltern der Erde (450 S.)
- Blüten des Lebensbaumes:
    - Die Struktur des kabbalistischen Lebensbaumes (370 S.)
    - Der kabbalistische Lebensbaum als Forschungshilfsmittel (580 S.)
    - Der kabbalistische Lebensbaum als spirituelle Landkarte (520 S.)

Die Themen der 87 Bände der Reihe „Die Götter der Germanen"

1. Die Entwicklung der germanischen Religion
2. Lexikon der germanischen Religion
3. Der ursprüngliche Göttervater Tyr
4. Tyr in der Unterwelt: der Schmied Wieland
5. Tyr in der Unterwelt: der Riesenkönig   Teil 1
6. Tyr in der Unterwelt: der Riesenkönig   Teil 2
7. Tyr in der Unterwelt: der Zwergenkönig
8. Der Himmelswächter Heimdall
9. Der Sommergott Baldur
10. Der Meeresgott: Ägir, Hler und Njörd
11. Der Eibengott Ullr
12. Die Zwillingsgötter Alcis
13. Der neue Göttervater Odin   Teil 1
14. Der neue Göttervater Odin   Teil 2
15. Der Fruchtbarkeitsgott Freyr
16. Der Chaos-Gott Loki
17. Der Donnergott Thor
18. Der Priestergott Hönir
19. Die Göttersöhne
20. Die unbekannteren Götter
21. Die Göttermutter Frigg
22. Die Liebesgöttin: Freya und Menglöd
23. Die Erdgöttinnen
24. Die Korngöttin Sif
25. Die Apfel-Göttin Idun
26. Die Hügelgrab-Jenseitsgöttin Hel
27. Die Meeres-Jenseitsgöttin Ran
28. Die unbekannteren Jenseitsgöttinnen
29. Die unbekannteren Göttinnen
30. Die Nornen
31. Die Walküren
32. Die Zwerge
33. Der Urriese Ymir
34. Die Riesen
35. Die Riesinnen
36. Mythologische Wesen
37. Mythologische Priester und Priesterinnen
38. Sigurd/Siegfried
39. Helden und Göttersöhne
40. Die Symbolik der Vögel und Insekten
41. Die Symbolik der Schlangen, Drachen und Ungeheuer
42.a Die Symbolik der Herdentiere I
42.b Die Symbolik der Herdentiere II
43. Die Symbolik der Raubtiere
44. Die Symbolik der Wassertiere und sonstigen Tiere
45. Die Symbolik der Pflanzen
46. Die Symbolik der Farben
47. Die Symbolik der Zahlen
48. Die Symbolik von Sonne, Mond und Sternen
49.a Das Jenseits I – Das Hügelgrab
49.b Das Jenseits II – Der Jenseitsweg
50. Seelenvogel, Utiseta und Einweihung
51. Wiederzeugung und Wiedergeburt
52. Elemente der Kosmologie
53. Der Weltenbaum
54. Die Symbolik der Himmelsrichtungen und der Jahreszeiten
55.a Mythologische Motive I
55.b Mythologische Motive II
56. Der Tempel
57. Die Einrichtung des Tempels
58. Priesterin – Seherin – Zauberin – Hexe
59. Priester – Seher – Zauberer
60. Rituelle Kleidung und Schmuck
61. Skalden und Skaldinnen
62. Kriegerinnen und Ekstase-Krieger
63. Die Symbolik der Körperteile
64.a Magie und Ritual I
64.b Magie und Ritual II
64.c Magie und Ritual III
65. Gestaltwandlungen
66.a Magische Angriffs-Waffen
66.b Magische Verteidigungs-Waffen
67. Magische Werkzeuge und Gegenstände
68. Zaubersprüche
69. Göttermet
70. Zaubertränke
71. Träume, Omen und Orakel
72. Runen
73. Sozial-religiöse Rituale
74. Weisheiten und Sprichworte
75. Kenningar
76. Rätsel
77. Die vollständige Edda des Snorri Sturluson
78. Frühe Skaldenlieder
79.a Mythologische Sagas I
79.b Mythologische Sagas II
80. Hymnen an die germanischen Götter

76